'Such an important book on a vi  [
We are all built for relationship [
This book wonderfully highligh [
the need for us to connect well and to prioritise relationships,
read it and live it. A real book for our times.'
Gavin Calver, CEO, Evangelical Alliance

'Loneliness is at an epidemic level today. Even those of us who know
lots of people can feel that our relationships aren't of the quality we'd
like. Phil Knox helps us to understand these feelings and provides
helpful and realistic steps, enabling us to grow in more satisfying
friendships – not only with one another, but also with the living God.'
Peter Dray, Director, Creative Evangelism, UCCF: The Christian
Unions

'As we work to see change in our streets and communities, there are
few things more important than friendships. They are the relational
glue that hold us together. Phil is such a wordsmith and has written
a great book full of humour and wisdom that will help us all to
deepen our friendships and expand our networks. It is a ray of hope
that explores how we can thrive in our relationships and be the best
of friends to those around us. I'm praying it has a huge impact.'
Debra Green OBE, Executive Director, Redeeming Our
Communities

'My dear friend Phil has penned a much-needed and brilliant book.
The reason this book is so good is because it is written by someone
who, quite frankly, is brilliant at being a friend – to those who are
believers and those who aren't. Full of research, story, insight and the
Bible, this book will inspire your existing friendships as well as those
yet to be formed. I am beyond excited to encourage you to read it.'
Mark Greenwood, National Evangelist and Head of Evangelism,
Elim Pentecostal Churches UK

'This book is relevant, timely and a reminder that we are not made to live on an island by ourselves. We were made to be relational. We need friends.'
Les Isaac OBE, President, Ascension Trust

'We all need friends, yet friendship is something we rarely think about. This thoughtful and thought-provoking book should help all of us to have richer, deeper and more lasting friendships and to use them to build God's kingdom. Invest time in reading this book; it will be amply repaid!'
The Revd Canon J.John

'I believe every human is created in God's image and, as such, deep relationships are hard-wired into us and are needed in order for us to reflect God in the world. There is a desperate need for us all to invest in meaningful, sacrificial relationships, and Phil has written a book that not only has a compelling argument but makes the process and steps needed to build new friendships outside our Christian bubbles easy and accessible to everyone.'
John Kirkby CBE, founder, Isaiah 61 Movement (i61m), and founder, Christians Against Poverty

'This is a book about friendship that explores why this biblical community value is so crucial – despite the age of technological and communications advancement, which still leaves us isolated. With the fragmentation, disintegration and dislocation of our Western world, which cherishes individualism, friendships rooted in God and community reflect a critical countercultural worldview. Humanity is relationally wired because our architect, God, made us to be like him; therefore, we long for connection. Phil has given us a template in this book for connecting with God so that we can learn how to connect with our world. Christians and non-Christians will find this book valuable.'
The Revd Dr Israel Oluwole Olofinjana, Director, One People Commission, Evangelical Alliance

'This book helps us to recognize the pressures that friendships face in our culture, yet lifts our vision to the God-given potential of all our friendships. Phil Knox distils valuable insights from academic research and everyday life, combining helpful frameworks with highly practical tips. Most importantly of all, we're brought back to our Creator God, and shown how our ordinary friendships are part of God's wonderful design for human beings, and how we can delight in finding the Best of Friends perfectly fulfilled in Jesus Christ.'
John Russell, Lead Minister, Cornerstone Church, Nottingham

'There is a wonderful moment in Phil's book, *The Best of Friends*, when he tells us about the time he and his wife Dani bought their first house. They decided to "mark their territory" by scribbling their names on the hallway wall. Fourteen years later, that same wall is covered with the names of friends and family who have eaten there, stayed there, popped in for a visit or just come over for a chat.

'Friendship . . . true friendship is *the* missing ingredient in so many of our lives and, in this extraordinary and thought-provoking book, you and I get to join Phil and Dani in understanding this powerful and life-transforming gift, and to learn how to put friendship to work in each of our daily lives.

'Do we have a place in our lives where other people get to imprint their names and some of their stories and leave a mark that lasts and lasts? That's friendship, and the world is crying out for this intimacy . . . to know and be known, to love and be loved, perhaps more than ever before.

'The next couple of years are probably going to be more challenging than most of us have prepared for. But if we have friends, then this season can still be one of beauty, closeness, love and laughter.

'Phil is a good friend. So let him walk with you through the pages of this book, as we each learn how to find better friends for ourselves, and to be the Best of Friends to those around us.'
Fergus Scarfe, Regional Director, GOD TV

'Now I know why the Quakers have the best name for a denomination: "Society of Friends". You *fall* in love, but you *make* friends. This is a book that is timely, challenging, convicting . . . a barnstormer of a book that shows us how to "make friends" like Jesus did.'
Leonard Sweet, author, professor, publisher and founder, <preachthestory.com>

'More and deeper friendships are the need of the hour. In *The Best of Friends*, Phil Knox brings key insights from the sciences into conversation with the life of Jesus to show how you and I can go beyond mere acquaintanceship to meaningful comradery. A recommended read for these disconnected times.'
Sheridan Voysey, founder, <FriendshipLab.org>, presenter of *Pause for Thought*, BBC Radio 2, and author of *The Making of Us*

'Small children are great at making friends, but as adults we've often lost the knack. Phil Knox helps us to consider what friendship is for, how it works and why it matters. He helps us to explore Jesus' model of friendship and see what we can learn from it as we navigate our own relationships. This book will encourage you to be more thankful for the friendships you have, and more intentional about maintaining and developing them.'
Kate Wharton, Vicar, St Bart's Roby, Assistant National Leader, New Wine England, and author of *Single-Minded*

'Phil has done a great job of writing a book that speaks to us in this present moment. After the forced disconnection of the Covid years, the content of this book is so relevant and timely.

'It's well written and made me laugh at times, tear up at times and, most of all, appreciate afresh the importance of friendships. Phil encourages us and equips us all for living intentional lives of relational richness. This is a book that needs to be widely read.'
Ness Wilson, Leader, Pioneer UK

Phil Knox is an evangelist, speaker and missiologist at the Evangelical Alliance. He is passionate about making Jesus known and seeing communities thrive. He loves learning and has degrees in law and mission and evangelism. Phil is married to Dani and they have two sons, Caleb and Jos. He is an avid runner, enthusiastic waterskier and once broke the world record for the longest five-a-side football match. He is also a performance poet and the author of *Story Bearer*. *The Best of Friends* is his second book.

THE BEST OF FRIENDS

THE BEST OF FRIENDS

Choose wisely, care well

Phil Knox

INTER-VARSITY PRESS
36 Causton Street, London SW1P 4ST, England
Email: ivp@ivpbooks.com
Website: www.ivpbooks.com

First published 2023

British Library Cataloguing-in-Publication Data
A catalogue record for this book is available from the British Library.

ISBN: 978–1–78974–424–8
eBook ISBN: 978–1–78974–425–5

Set in Minion Pro 10.25/13.75pt
Typeset in Great Britain by CRB Associates, Potterhanworth, Lincolnshire
Printed in Great Britain by Ashford Colour Press Ltd, Gosport, Hampshire

Produced on paper from sustainable sources

*Inter-Varsity Press publishes Christian books that are true to the Bible and that
communicate the gospel, develop discipleship and strengthen the church for its mission
in the world.*

*IVP originated within the Inter-Varsity Fellowship, now the Universities and Colleges
Christian Fellowship, a student movement connecting Christian Unions in universities and
colleges throughout Great Britain, and a member movement of the International Fellowship
of Evangelical Students. Website: www.uccf.org.uk. That historic association is maintained,
and all senior IVP staff and committee members subscribe to the UCCF Basis of Faith.*

To Dani and Adam, the best of friends

Contents

Foreword

When Phil told me he had written another book and that this one was all about friendship, my immediate reaction was to laugh. Not at Phil, not at the project; it wasn't that kind of laughter. It was the kind of knowing chuckle of someone walking through their front door thinking they're getting home early to plan a surprise for their housemates, only to discover there's a party of friends already inside who have beaten them to the same idea.

I was delighted to hear the news. Delighted and amused because, as I told Phil in response, I had said to God and to a publisher friend only a few months earlier that, were I to write a book in these days, it would have to be on friendship. The lost art of making true, deep, joyful friendships. The glory and the grit of sticking with people over decades. The vital importance of having friends: not just lovers or family or contacts or followers, but true friends.

Then Phil went and beat me to it and also did a much better job than I could have done. As I say, I am genuinely delighted. And I am proud of my friend for the brilliant book he has written.

Phil is probably the most upbeat and consistently encouraging person I know. Out of this man's mouth come words of life, time and time again. He embodies such passion and energy that you end up feeling more alive just from being around him. However, he's not just enthusiasm. He's a researcher, he's a reader and he's a practical theologian. He lives the stuff, he tries it at home and he sticks at it until he finds what works, sees fruit begin to sprout or learns a better way.

Phil is also really good friends with Jesus. This makes a world of difference in what he's writing and why. He's working with the best of friends. In the church we really don't talk about friendship enough, if at all. Yet Jesus calls friendship the highest form of love and celebrates it: 'My command is this: Love each other as I have loved you. Greater love has no one than this: to lay down one's life for one's friends' (John 15:12–13).

It amazes me to see the amount of focus we still give to romance, marriage, parenting and even evangelism and justice work, all the while not talking about the lay-your-life-down love that's found in true friendship. A love that is surely needed in every facet of relating to one another. The fact that Phil is friends with Jesus, the ultimate friend, means that even though he won't be the world's leading friendship expert (because who is?), he is learning from the best. They talk. They love each other. The friend that is Jesus is also showing up in these pages. That is good news for us all.

As more stats and headlines continue to be released over the coming years on just how lonely and disconnected people are becoming in this age of constant connection, I think this book is a tonic. Reading it felt tangibly refreshing to me. I think I have been hungry for good, rich writing on friendship and loving others well, over the popular stream of content on leadership, effectiveness in the workplace or even self-help.

What a joy to get to think about our friends and focus on the wonderful, irreplaceable gift that friendship is made to be for each of us. And what a relief to discover there are practical steps we can take towards being the best of friends and knowing the God of the universe as the best of friends with us, every step of the way.

Thank you, Phil, my friend, for bringing this book to the world. I'm really glad you wrote it!

Miriam Swanson
Director, Fusion USA

Acknowledgments

When you write a book about friendship, one of the beautiful things is that it is shaped in some way by each and every friend you have ever had. These pages belong to you: they are your story too.

To my inner circle – Dani, Adam, Debs, Ste – thank you for sticking by me in the valley and celebrating with me on the mountaintop. Thank you for listening to the frightened child within me and reminding me of my shoe size when I've got too big for my boots.

To my wider circles – the rich tapestry drawn from family, school, university, church, work, summer camps – I am indebted to your love, care, example, encouragement and presence in my life. This book is a credit to you all and I am forever grateful for the gift you are to me.

This book exists because of an all-star cast. Thank you to my boss Jo Frost, who encouraged me to develop as a writer, and thanks also for the relentless inspiration of the team at the Evangelical Alliance – let's keep changing the world together. To my agent, Tony Collins, whose 'kick up the backside' propelled this book into life and whose extraordinary expertise and tenacity shaped it at a formative stage. To my editor Tom Creedy, whose pursuit of excellence and sharp theological mind have honed and finetuned this work to completion. To the rest of the IVP and SPCK team, it's an honour to work with you.

Finally, to the very best of friends, the one who sticks closer than a brother, King Jesus: this book is for you. May it bring you glory and may we look more like the friends you made us to be as a result of reading it.

Enterlude

We need friends.

We've got music and movies on demand.
We've got the world in the palm of our hand.
We've got fun trips, internships, play scripts and hair snips,
film clips, fish and chips, at the touch of our thumb tips.
Need to lead or breed or feed your cat?
Well, it turns out there's an app for that.
But we need friends.

We've got computers for a fiver,
Cars without a driver.
We've got louder, faster, further, more,
A bigger network than ever before,
But we need friends.

And friends are amazing.
See, friendship is atomic.
From the boardroom to the nursing home,
from the coffee shop to the playground,
It's relational connections that make the world go round.
We were created to know and be known.
It's better to eat kebabs with friends than salad on your own.

And yet we trace in populous places, we're strangers in rooms
    of familiar faces.
We crave deep and meaningfuls but experience anonymity.
We dance superficially around the promise of proximity.

And we need friends.
And quantity is no substitute for quality.

We need 5G-, HD-, 24-carat friends,
Lifelong, fight-strong, tag-along, forgive-all-wrongs friends.
Friends to talk through our problems personal.
Friends to call when the cancer's terminal.

And look to the one who makes friendship possible,
Whose nail-pierced hands bridged a chasm uncrossable.
His scandalous invitation follows the most glorious of
    amends.
There is no greater love than they that lay down their life for
    their friends.

So celebrate with me the ship most worth sailing,
And follow the example of the friend unfailing.
May we raise our game and drop our cover,
Invest our energies in one another.
May we still be there when the rain starts to fall,
And accept the most important friend request of all

Because we need friends.

Introduction

Greater love has no one than this: to lay down one's life for one's friends.
(John 15:13)

Mrs Passmore's class still remember the day Juggling Johnny strode into the assembly hall. Thirty cross-legged, straight-backed, usually fidgety 7-year-olds were glued to their allotted square of wooden hall floor, spellbound by the mysterious guest. Without introduction, the colourfully dressed entertainer began to place upright garden canes at the feet of the front row of the infant audience. Eyes widened and mouths gaped as Johnny pulled a white ceramic plate from his suitcase and demonstrably displayed it to his expectant crowd. So it began . . .

The first two plates began spinning effortlessly and were welcomed by 'oohs' and 'ahhhs'. But this appreciative audience were about to discover how under-prepared this part-time conjurer was. Further plates went on poles – three, four, five, six – and by this stage Mrs Passmore would have been able to see the tension etched across Juggling Johnny's face. He frantically raced between the canes, before fatally attempting a seventh item of crockery. The naive young minds in front of him probably believed all might still end well, but this fragile belief was about to come crashing down around them, along with the plates.

In the immediate aftermath – despite some children still covering their ears and shuffling back from the makeshift stage, a despairing Mrs Passmore and a sheepish Johnny – my classmate David Wilson, who was sitting next to me, shouted, 'Miss, can I have a go?'

When it comes to the state of our friendships, most of us are either Juggling Johnny or David Wilson. Many of us are spinning friendships, desperately trying to maintain enough of a connection with an ever-widening network of contacts. Perpetuated by a never-ending stream of messages flashing up on our phones, we dash between circles of friends and family members, afraid that if we don't stay in touch, the relationship will come crashing to the floor. Some of us, on the other hand, feel achingly lonely, as if we are watching a world of intimate connections that we are missing out on. Like my friend David, all we want is one plate to spin.

Was friendship really meant to be this way? Especially with the advanced communication devices at our thumb tips, surely there is a way to navigate the world of relationships that doesn't leave us feeling overwhelmed or isolated, guilty or lonely?

This is a book about friendship. It is a celebration of how profoundly good it is to know and be known. It is a timely reminder that in the age of infinite connection, where contact with almost anyone on the planet is but a few clicks away, the pursuit of deep, close, intimate relationships really matters, and does not happen by accident.

This is a book about community. It is a rallying cry to throw ourselves into interdependent and diverse groups of people and church families in a society that is becoming increasingly fragmented. It is a challenge to find our identity not solely from within ourselves but from the God who made us and the company he has placed us in. It is a counter-cultural call to arms to stand against the relentless narrative of individualism and live in a way that invites others to be welcomed into life-enhancing relational connections.

And this is a book about God. Our primary subject matter can only be adequately explored by getting to know the One who conceived, constructed and consecrated friendship itself. What is extraordinary is that not only does God *establish* friendship, but he *embodies* it. In the coming chapters we will learn about what great connection looks like from its very creator and celebrate his invitation to love and be loved.

There is nothing like friendship.

We ache to connect and be connected.

But friendships are made, not born. Relationships take time, hard work, heartache and perseverance. We need to talk more about how we decide who to befriend and how we forge our most important connections. Author and pastor Kevin DeYoung agrees: 'Have you ever noticed we seldom study friendship? It is the most important least talked about relationship in the church.'[1]

This is a conversation for our age and a conversation for the ages. Friendship is a timely and timeless subject matter. On one hand, the subject matter needs urgent discussion. In a world still reeling from the impact of a global pandemic, the landscape of relationship has changed. During the various lockdowns, many of the incidental friendships we took for granted, those with people we used to see regularly at church or work, have diminished or died entirely. For some, social distancing meant social isolation. Many in our society are lonelier. Alongside this bad news, many of the intentional friendships we have invested in during Covid-19 have flourished and thrived. We have got to know our neighbours better. We will remember who was there for us when we look back on this chapter in our stories. In a post-pandemic world, we need to talk about what friendship looks like in the years ahead.

On the other hand, this subject has enduring relevance. We humans are relationally wired. Our need for companions and companionship has been central to art and literature since the dawn of civilization. We have always been fascinated by how we relate to one another and sought to understand how to do it better. We should continue to do so; that's why we are embarking on this journey to be the best of friends.

Our journey takes place in five stages. First, we will immerse ourselves in the subject matter and take a deep dive into the power of friendship. We will consider what it is about us that hardwires us for connection and why we yearn to walk with others on life's pilgrimage from the playground to the retirement home. Second, we will identify the pressures on friendship and ask why something so good can be so difficult and painful. Third, we'll consider the various circles of friends in which we find ourselves. We will explore the patterns and principles upon which Jesus structured his relationships, because we need to learn from the best how to invest our time and emotions in our immediate connections. Fourth, we will consider intergenerational friendship and discover the potential of connections across the ages, before fifth, talking about the most important friendship of all.

Each of the main chapters is titled with a number or a mathematical symbol. I am not a great mathematician; in fact, my lack of flair for the subject was probably a great disappointment to my late mum, who was a maths teacher. Each number or symbol corresponds to the size of the relational circle we are exploring. Most of the core chapters conclude with some intensely practical tips and pieces of advice for putting the principles into practice.

I also write as someone who hasn't got this friendship thing sorted. Your author is a wholehearted friend and relationship enthusiast who is still working things out, making new connections and fresh mistakes in equal measure. But I am convinced that after hundreds of conversations and in-depth exploration of scientific, sociological and theological research, this is a conversation we desperately need to have.

This is a book for you. I don't know anyone who claims to be the perfect friend. We all have room to grow as we learn to dance our way through the ever-changing friendship circles in which we find ourselves and are found. We could all do with a bit of help. Even the most introverted among us cannot sustain ourselves solely with the energy of our own company. The most gregarious of us need a different kind of help; to ask questions about quality of friendship over quantity.

Consider this an invitation to travel with me through the various circles, celebrating the friends you have and considering the friends you need. We spend hours investing time in improving our golf swings, developing DIY skills, learning languages, becoming a better cook, runner or leader. There are over 10,000 books with 'leadership' in the title. By comparison only a fraction contain the word 'friendship'. Cheesy, I know, but friendship is the 'ship' I want to sail.

My hope is that reading this book will help you to be the best of friends. What if friendship is the key to healing the divisions that are fracturing our communities, families, churches, streets and societies? My prayer is that fewer people will be lonely, neighbours smile at each other, relationships plumb new depths, the good news travels faster, churches grow, and all of us can bask in the delight of one of God's greatest gifts to us.

I hope that by the time you place this book on the coffee table in front of you, having turned the last page and recommended it to a friend, you simply love those around you more, understand better how to relate to them and put the Creator of connection at the heart of your friendship circles.

Let's get started, shall we?

Surprisingly enough, *The Best of Friends* is a book that is best enjoyed journeying with others. To that end I have designed some small-group resources with discussion questions and fun activities to enhance and apply the learning from the book. You can find these along with supplementary videos and more at: www.philknox.co.uk

1

The power of friendship

The greatest gift of life is friendship, and I have received it.
(Hubert H. Humphrey)

Friends

The late 1990s were my early teenage years. This means that every Friday night, along with most of my peers, I would curl up on a sofa in Central Perk with six twenty-something New Yorkers. It means that most people born within a decade of me have a strong opinion of whether or not Ross and Rachel were on a break. It also means I can never carry a sofa anywhere without shouting 'Pivot!'. A generation came of age observing the power of relationship while watching *Friends*. (If you missed it, you can spend the small matter of 5,191 minutes of your life catching up on the ten seasons.)

This immensely popular TV sitcom is so well loved for a number of reasons (despite finishing in 2004, it was still the favourite TV programme for young people in the UK in 2019[1]), but at the heart of it is the sheer power and dynamism of friendship. In this chapter we will consider why friendship is *so* powerful. What is it about our connection to others that matters so much to us and what are its effects? Why would former US president Woodrow Wilson say with such confidence, 'Friendship is the only cement that will hold the world together'?[2]

Back to the start

We can trace the source of the potency of relationship back to the first pages of the Bible. The book of Genesis describes the creation of the cosmos. From chapter 1 we begin to see clues of a creator who, although acting as one, is doing so in three persons, a mystery Christians call God the Trinity. These persons are all present at creation. In just the second verse we read that 'the *Spirit of God* was hovering over the waters' (emphasis added). In verse 26 it is noticeable that God says, 'Let us make mankind in *our* image' (emphasis added). The three-in-one God is creating collectively.

This beautiful mystery runs like a heartbeat through the Old Testament and becomes explicit in the New. For example, John, at the outset of his masterful telling of Jesus' story, echoes the words of Genesis and declares, 'In the beginning was the Word' (John 1:1). This Word is Jesus, there from the beginning. Paul is even more explicit: 'in him all things were created: things in heaven and on earth, visible and invisible' (Colossians 1:16). When we put these jigsaw pieces together, we have a complete picture of Father, Son and Holy Spirit, all active when the world was woven together. Galaxies, giraffes, grasslands and goldfish were created out of the overflow of this relationship between the Trinity.

God wants us to know that intimacy is at the heart of his intention from square one. Before the curtain is raised on creation, there is a conversation going on backstage. As author and pastor Jonathan Holmes observes: 'The Trinity is the most fundamental expression of community and relationship. Therefore, one of the simplest yet most profound aspects of mankind being made in God's image is that we were designed to live in relationships.'[3]

We carry the indelible imprint of our designer.

But there is more to come as the universe takes shape. The first couple of chapters tell us at regular intervals that the Creator takes stock and repeatedly ponders his workmanship with satisfaction, with the refrain, 'God saw that it was good.' When the work is complete an additional adverb is inserted to emphasize an even more complete sense of contentment: 'It was *very* good.' Eight times the Creator appreciates the virtues of what he has made before stating, in a way that might surprise the reader, that something is *not* good. Having been so delighted with the events thus far, what could possibly be less than perfect?

'It is not good for the man to be alone' (Genesis 2:18).[4]

The Beatles sang that all we need is love. I saw an advert recently that ambitiously claimed, 'All you need is cake.' There are also a few Christian worship songs that contain lyrics with an overwhelming sentiment that 'all you need is Jesus'. I sympathize with the heart behind words that encourage the singer towards expressing complete dependence on God, but that's not what God originally said about our fundamental need. It is not good for man to be alone; in other words, we need friends. We were created for friendship.

The science of friendship

The statement 'We were created for friendship' can be scientifically proven. When we make friends, get to know people better and spend time with those we love, our fearfully and wonderfully made bodies remind us that this is what we were created for. Our brains secrete one of the Creator's most powerful inventions: a hormone that goes by the name of oxytocin.

Oxytocin is most people's favourite chemical. When you are sitting around a campfire on a summer's evening and you experience an inexplicable feeling of connection to those around you as you talk and laugh over rising, glowing embers, that is oxytocin doing its work. When a friend opens up over a cup of coffee, you say your goodbyes and then experience a warm and fuzzy feeling that you have bonded to another level with that individual, your blood is streaming with 'the cuddle chemical'. When you reach that point in a relationship where you are ready to trust someone with long-held secrets or the invitation to turn up and let themselves into your home unannounced, you have reached peak oxytocin.

And the presence of oxytocin is long lasting. It's evidence of the power of enduring friendship. It's the reason why, when wrinkled hands shake after decades of connection, there is an infinitely stronger bond than between the teenagers who have just shared their first sleepover.

The second substance at the party is cortisol. This hormone plays a completely different role from oxytocin, but its presence can be heavily influenced by those around us. Its importance to our internal bodily functions cannot be overstated. Almost every cell contains cortisol receptors. It helps regulate our blood pressure and blood sugar levels. It serves the immune and digestive systems and prepares us for action. This function of preparing us for action means that our cortisol levels rise when we are stressed. If you were thinking by my description so far that cortisol is not the most relational substance, you would be right, but its relationship with friendship is important. In fact, it's a matter of life and death.

Several studies have explored the difference that the quality of our connections have on cortisol levels.[5] These studies find that if you don't have a close friend, your cortisol levels increase significantly. Those with a best friend experience less dramatic changes to levels of the hormone in their blood stream. What does this mean? How might this impact our health?

When our levels of cortisol are consistently high, it's as if we are preparing our bodies to face a non-existent threat. Our senses are on red alert. Physiologically, more and more sugar is released in the blood, which can damage our pancreas and increase the risk of diabetes. It then narrows our arteries to get blood to organs and muscles faster, but raises the likelihood of cardiac arrest. Worse still, bodily resources are drawn away from core biological business, meaning we are more vulnerable to illness. Cortisol is perfect for getting us out of bed and out of danger, but when we consistently overdose on it, it can be seriously bad for our health. And that is what friendship saves us from.

Robin Dunbar, an anthropologist and friendship guru, identifies another key player. He links our time spent with companions and the activities of friendship to the release of endorphins. These neuro-chemicals are the body's natural pain-relief system and are activated when we do many of the things that we do in the presence of others: laughing, singing, dancing . . . and hugging! They don't just make us feel good; they also stimulate the release of natural white blood cells, which strengthen our body's defences and increase our immunity to disease.[6]

That is the scientific, biological, neurological power of friendship. Relationship is seriously good for us. We are hardwired in our bodies for connection. And in equal measure, it seems there are dire consequences from being disconnected.

Friends with benefits

More than ever before we are talking about our well-being. In the UK, almost a third of young adults aged 18–24 feel hopeless.[7] Almost a fifth of those aged 16–25 do not believe that life is worth living.[8] Over a quarter say that their lives have no purpose. The interaction between our emotional and relational health is an urgent conversation.

In part because of the neurological reasons given above, we should not be surprised that the factor distinguishing the happiest 10% of people from everyone else is the strength of their social relationships.[9] There is something so good about getting to know people, spending time with them and engaging with each other on a deep level that profoundly impacts our physical, emotional and spiritual health. Here's Robin Dunbar again:

> Friendship protects us from disease as well as cognitive decline, allows us to be more engaged with the tasks that we have to do, and helps us to become more embedded within, and trusting of, the wider community within which we live.[10]

And the depth of these friendships is important. The more we talk with friends, the happier we are. But it is those who regularly engage in meaningful conversation that report the highest levels of happiness and well-being.[11]

Perhaps our increasing tendency to separate body, mind and soul, and deny entirely the existence of a spiritual component to our lives, has played down the significance of our friendships for our overall well-being. As we have promoted and enthroned individualism as one of the gods of our age, conversations about health have sometimes been limited to 'eat less, move more'. Clearly on a purely physical level this is broadly sound advice if we want to lose weight, but when we look at the evidence, a much more holistic approach screams at us from the pages of research. Studies consistently show that those who eat unhealthily, smoke, drink heavily and lack exercise, but have strong friendships, live significantly longer than those who look after themselves physically but are socially isolated.

It really is better to eat kebabs with friends than a salad on your own.

The proof of the pudding

A fascinating case study demonstrates the power of strong relational bonds in extending life expectancy. In the 1950s, researchers began to be baffled by an American town called Roseto, where mortality rates were a third lower than in the rest of the United States. Signs of heart disease were non-existent in younger generations, and in the elderly they were a fraction of what was observed across the surrounding towns and cities. The first thing the academics looked at was the lifestyle of the town. Were they a community of health freaks?

If anything, they treated their physical well-being with the same level of care a wet Labrador applies to a freshly washed duvet. They smoked heavy-duty cigars, fried their sausages and meatballs in lard and drank wine with abandon. Their strong hearts were nothing to do with salads and protein shakes.

Their secret power was their connectivity. Rosetan households contained three to four generations. This was a community where everybody knew everybody. The ties of trust and friendship ran deep. Food, faith and problems were shared between families and age groups. A biopsy of the average resident would have found soaring levels of oxytocin and record lows of cortisol. This is the power of relationship at work. Friendship is seriously good for your health. It turns out that the secret of eternal life is not about what you know but who you know.

Does that sound familiar?

Friendship is powerful because God gives it

The virtues of health and well-being are sizeable but are far from the main reason we should make friendship a priority. People are worthy of our time, energy and attention because friendship is God's gift to us. It is his creation, his passion and his purpose for our lives. The reason it is so powerful, so beneficial and so beautiful is that it has divine instigation, ordination and benediction.

All the physical, mental and emotional benefits of relational connection are magnificent, but they are not the primary reason to pursue deep communion with friends. We should prioritize friendship because it is God's gift to us, and he invites us to take hold of it with both hands. Community is the place in which God created us to dwell. Relationship is the train he invites us to board.

From Genesis to Revelation, from the garden to the heavenly city, we see real people in real relationship. We often remember the exploits of biblical heroes without giving due kudos to their supporting cast. Take David. His life was the supreme example of courage in the face of a giant, patience in realizing a calling, humility in recovering and repenting from sin, leadership in war and peacetime, and adoration of the God he served. Yet without a mentor in Samuel, a loyal friend in Jonathan, an editor in Nathan, a protégé in Solomon, not to mention the thirty-seven 'mighty men', he might never have defeated Goliath, presided over spectacular military victories, reigned during Israel's golden age and brought glory to God in the way that he did. Abraham had Lot, Naomi had Ruth, Elijah had Elisha, Daniel had Shadrach, Meshach and Abednego, Paul had Barnabas: Scripture is scattered with friendships that make the difference.

Friendship is God's irreplaceable gift to us.

Soul mates

This gift of God goes beyond extending physical life and enhancing emotional well-being; the relational deity has created a world in which our connection to him is intrinsically linked to our web of relationships. One historic confession of faith, the Westminster Shorter Catechism, famously declares that the 'chief end of man' is to 'glorify God, and to enjoy him for ever'. It would be easy to think in our highly individualized world that we could achieve this 'end' on our own. The reality is that the journey of faith is a team game, not an individual pursuit. It is no coincidence that when Jesus tells us that all the law and prophets hang on the commandment to love God with heart, soul and mind, he immediately combines it with the instruction to love your neighbour as yourself. The two are inseparable. The Greatest Commandment is a great co-mandate. We glorify God by the way we treat those around us, and we worship him, follow him, get to know him and become more like him together.

Just as our physical lifespan is contracted by social seclusion, going solo spiritually will threaten to squeeze the spiritual life out of us if we find ourselves isolated as disciples.

I've seen this repeatedly in the lives of others. I met Mark on a dance floor as a student. It was clear he'd had a few beers. I saw him coming. He approached me unsteadily before reaching into his shirt to pull out a cross on the end of a gold chain that hung around his neck. 'I hear you are one of these,' he said, shouting over the music and pointing at the piece of jewellery. 'We should talk.' A couple of days later in a quieter environment we chatted. Mark had been at university for a few weeks, and explained he was struggling a little as a Christian. We became good friends. He found a church family who loved him, and he committed to them. He's a wholehearted Jesus-follower today. Without community and relationship, I do not believe his story would have been the same.

I observed this in another friend, Liam. Liam became a Christian after a dramatic series of events, and his first weeks were full of the miraculous and a deep dive into the Bible, worship and church. I'm not sure he could have had a better start. But then after a couple of months, his circumstances changed and he found himself in a new town, making new connections. He was equipped with an armoury of Christian books, music and resources, but he didn't find a church. Although I saw Liam a few times during this period, I'm not sure I did my best to help him. I gave advice, tried to encourage him, but I wish I had done more to challenge him to find a Christian community to journey with and do life with. Liam gave up on God not long after this.

It makes complete sense that our primary pursuit – to know and love God – should be inseverable from our relational connections with one another. We cannot go it alone.

A formative moment in the life of the founder of Methodism, John Wesley, came when an unknown, unnamed 'serious man' came to him and advised him with these true and profound words: 'Sir, you wish to serve God and go to heaven? Remember that you cannot serve him alone. You must therefore find companions or make them. The Bible knows nothing of solitary religion.'[12]

Friendship has the power to save and sustain our spiritual walk.

It is not good for man to be alone.

Right here, right now

As well as being a timeless necessity in our lives, in cultural terms friendship is fast becoming the most significant type of relationship. Sociologists, observing generational shifts, began noticing that friends were replacing family and romantic partners in the relational pecking order. Here is author Rebecca Huntley, writing in 2006 about Generation Y (those born between 1982 and 2000): 'Friends come first because unlike your family and your current relationship, they are the ones you can count on in the long run.'[13]

This trend is a fascinating one and shows no sign of letting up. With around a third of all UK marriages sadly ending in divorce, and couples increasingly likely to delay getting married and many not choosing to do so at all, younger generations are experiencing fragile family lives. In contrast, friendship is seen more and more as a solid relational foundation. Family is far from being abandoned, but especially as the pace of change threatens to create even more distance between the generations, the prominence of friendship is here to stay. Megan Garber comments: 'Long conceived as side dishes to the main feast – marriage, kids, the nuclear family above all – friendships, more and more, are helping to define people's sense of themselves in the world.'[14]

From the first of our forefathers and mothers, we have needed each other. But, right now, as a society today we are facing complexities in the fabric of our families and rubric of relationships that would have been inconceivable and incomprehensible to our ancestors. The power of friendship has always mattered, but arguably it has never mattered more than now.

I hope that after reading this chapter you are left in no doubt as to the atomic fundamental of our connection with one another. I hope you take a moment to celebrate the life-giving and life-extending lifelines that your friends are to you, and the gift of life your friendship gives to them. I hope you are inspired to read on and wrestle with the themes of the coming chapters and picture yourself in the friendship circles we stand on the verge of exploring. But before we press on too quickly, we need to be aware of the dangers that threaten to ambush this critical journey, and to remind us of these we are heading back briefly to the miraculous town of Roseto.

The tragedy of returning to the small Pennsylvanian town in the twenty-first century is that the secret sauce has been taken out of the recipe. Today the signs of heart disease reflect the national average, and life expectancy is comparatively unremarkable. What happened? From the mid-1960s, the life-extending practices began to dwindle. Grandparents no longer lived in houses with their grandchildren. The Rosetans worked longer hours and had less time to build the strong relational ties. The cohesive, traditional way of life began to resemble the patterns of the rest of America. The distinctives that protected them from chronic illness had been eroded away. The Roseto Effect, it seems, was as vulnerable to the threats that all of our relationships face today. We turn to these now as we examine the pressure on friendship.

The themes of this chapter can be explored further using small-group resources, videos and discussion questions. Delve deeper at: www.philknox.co.uk

Further reading

J. Frost and P. Lynas, *Being Human* (Hodder and Stoughton, London, 2023). A beautiful and thorough unpacking of our humanity through a biblical lens, containing brilliant insight into contemporary culture and including an emphasis on human connection and relationship.

V. Roberts, *True Friendship* (10Publishing, Leyland, 2013). A scriptural guide as rich in practical advice as it is in biblical wisdom.

D. Smith, *God's Plan for Your Wellbeing* (CWR, Farnham, Surrey, 2020). Dave's 50-day guide is helpful across all six areas of well-being that he identifies, but for the section on relational well-being alone it is worth investing in this book.

2

The pressure on friendship

A perverse person stirs up conflict, and a gossip separates close friends.
(Proverbs 16:28)

If friendship is so powerful, so beneficial and so natural, why is this book even necessary? Surely these life-giving relationships should be at the front and centre of our lives?

A recent YouGov survey found that 18% of men and 12% of women do not have even one close friend.[1] This means that millions of people in our communities have no-one to call when they receive great news, no-one to sit down and talk to about important things, no-one to cry out to when a devastating storm arrives on the shores of life.

In the wake of a global virus ravaging our world, there is another pathogen that has us in its grip. Loneliness is an epidemic. During Covid-19 the proportion of people saying they 'often or always feel lonely' increased from 1 in 20 to 1 in 14. Globally, a third of us experience regular feelings of loneliness.[2] When you consider the difference friendship makes in physical health, emotional well-being and spiritual benefit, this is a calamitous state of affairs for our world. Mother Teresa called loneliness 'the leprosy of the West', and in an age where technology means we are more connected than ever before, why is it that our relationships are under such threat?

It turns out that friendship is under fire.

I'm one of those people who get far too involved with TV dramas. Sadly, with the enforced early nights brought on by becoming a dad, my days of bingeing box-sets or streaming series are over, but in my 20s I would live and breathe each compelling plot line. Over a week of my life was spent watching the thrilling episodes of *24*, in which the counter-terrorism agent Jack Bauer would battle against time, multiple villains and often himself to literally save the day – each series takes place over the course of a twenty-four-hour period. Spoiler alert: in almost every series, one of the central dramatic themes is the threat of an enemy within. Tension is expertly interwoven through the narratives with a double agent constantly compromising and hampering the efforts of the good guys to stop the bomb going off.

Despite friendship's power to give us emotional, spiritual and even physical life, there are forces at work to deny its blessing in our lives. For Jack Bauer and his team of government agents, a crucial factor is knowing *who* they are fighting against. Both the external and internal threats need to be identified.

It's the same for us. Paul, writing to the church in Ephesus about their new life in Jesus, identifies three enemies of Christians that we have been saved from (Ephesians 2:2). These are:

- 'the ways of this world';
- 'the ruler of the kingdom of the air';
- 'the spirit who is now at work in those who are disobedient'.

These have been commonly paraphrased as 'the world, the flesh and the devil'.[3] As we have seen, friendship is a key element of God-given human flourishing. So it is no surprise that these three combine to wage war against our relationships with others. Let's examine them, along with their impact, in turn.

The world

Friends are not made or maintained in a vacuum. The context in which we find ourselves and the pressures under which we relate to each other are real and have a significant impact. The narrative throughout the Bible depicts a world in which conditions are hostile to the gospel, the people of God and the relationships between us. How might the waters we are forced to swim in at this cultural moment affect this particular area of our lives?

Time – the oxygen of friendship

My sixteenth summer will live long in the memory. I remember physically leaping out of the exam hall on a sweltering June afternoon and punching the air in celebration, scarcely able to contemplate the months of freedom that lay ahead of me. September's restart seemed light years away and weeks of carefree afternoons, lazy mornings, holidays and summer camps were spread tantalizingly in front of me.

A couple of decades on, looking back on that idyllic time brings waves of nostalgia crashing over me. The weeks merge together in a beautiful, sentimental mix and replay in my mind like a grainy old cinematic film captured on a camcorder. But their legacy lives on in more substantial ways than merely in my memory. I am still friends with the guys I shared those halcyon days with.

Four of us – Adam, Matt, Jon and myself – shared that era of our lives together. We co-starred on each other's storyboards in that particular chapter. Hours were spent playing football, climbing trees, listening to 80s rock music and laughing uncontrollably until we could do so no longer. By night, we would stay over at each other's houses and sneak out, pushing the boundaries of our newfound freedom. These 'night missions' became legendary. I still have no idea how we didn't get caught – my mum found out about them during

Adam's best-man's speech at my wedding. Fortunately, I had two weeks on honeymoon before I returned to face some questions about my teenage deception.

Over twenty years on, Adam and Jon are two of my best friends. Matt lives further away, but we see each other occasionally and within minutes the distance between us disappears. For the formation of these significant relationships in my life, that summer with its shared experiences at a memorable time was critical. And the irreplaceable, decisive and vital ingredient was time. Time is the oxygen of friendship. Spend enough time in someone's presence, with no agenda and enough conversation, and the magic of relationship begins to take effect.

Even the best of friends need time. Time is to relationship what oxygen is to fire. Starve even the most furious inferno of the gas it needs to burn and it fizzles out.

A challenge for most of us is that the vast majority of life is not spent in the same abundance of time I experienced in my sixteenth summer. For many of us, our friendships feel like the embers in the hearth at the end of the night, in need of time to revive them. We are in deficit and we know it. We find ourselves saying things like, 'Let's catch up soon!' while staring at a diary with very little blank space to make it happen.

Time flies. But where does it go?

Career change

It feels as though we should have more time than our ancestors. The fact that shopping is delivered to our door, machines wash our clothes and plates with ever-increasing speed and efficiency, and our food preparation happens more quickly, should mean we have more time for relationship.

Also, we are not working as many hours as those in previous generations. In the 1870s, the average number of annual working hours per worker in the UK was 2,755. Over the last 150 years it has steadily decreased to 1,670 in 2017.[4] What has changed significantly is the number of people working in a household. At the start of the twenty-first century two-thirds of mothers with dependent children were working. By 2019 this was three-quarters.[5] Perhaps the fact that many of us are working in the homes we are living in is a significant factor as to why we feel time is squeezed.

The nature of work has changed too. Peter Drucker coined the phrase 'knowledge worker' in the 1950s as a way of defining those whose work is primarily driven by their brains rather than their bodies. These workers are first and foremost in the business of finding, organizing, managing and analysing information, solving problems and generating ideas. This covers a vast range of the workforce: lawyers, accountants, IT workers, marketers, engineers, doctors, people-managers, teachers and more. These are the people who 'think for a living'. And knowledge workers are on the increase.

Throughout the twentieth century, the percentage of knowledge workers rose sharply. Today an estimated 42% of us would fit into this category in the UK[6] and over 1 billion worldwide.[7] Forbes declared that, with the enforced shift to home working during the Covid-19 pandemic, 2020 was the year of the knowledge worker.[8] And perhaps that is why we feel so hard pressed in this area. The same muscles we use to relate to one another are the ones that more and more of us are using at work, leaving us making withdrawals from an emotional bank account that is already in the red. Kevin DeYoung makes this observation of the difference between manual labour and knowledge work: 'You can work physically for 12 hours a day, 6 days a week for a lifetime with few ill effects, but mental strain has a huge impact on our bodies.'[9]

Where we work also affects our time. First, we are spending more time on the daily commute. Second, we are also far more likely to move around the country or even the world when we change job. Pastor and author Vaughan Roberts comments, 'Continuity in where you live and work is rare these days with many moving from job to job and place to place throughout their lives.'[10] With ever-changing neighbours and workmates when we move home, job, school, club and church, many of us press reset on finding and forming friendships. If we know we won't be sticking around in a certain location for very long, we are far less likely to make the effort to get to know new people. Author Jon Yates finds:

> People who plan to leave somewhere in the next 5 years are 20–25% less likely to get involved in voluntary activities, attend religious activities, join a club. Transience changes too the behaviour of those who stay put. They too are less likely to get involved with voluntary activities.[11]

All these changes to our working patterns have an impact on the quality of our friendships and frequency of contact with companions.

The screen-agers

But it is not just our work that is having an impact on our sociability. The way we spend our leisure time has profoundly changed in the last 100 years and this too is influencing our friendships.

I've just done a quick calculation. In my house there are eight screens. That's two for each inhabitant, and the youngest cannot yet put on his own coat. Even when you take away the time spent looking at computer screens for work, we spend a significant proportion of our day watching football and films on TV, watching life-hack videos on laptops, and trawling through newsfeeds on our phones.

Technology is amazing. It is remarkable to have even been alive during the digital revolution and experience first-hand the extraordinary leaps of progress in our lifetime. What on earth did we do before we could order a taxi, a takeaway or a tuxedo at the touch of our thumb tips? It blows my children's minds when I tell them there were only four TV channels available when I was growing up.

And relationally, there are significant benefits. Whenever I ask a room of people what they love about social media, the first answer invariably given is the opportunities it gives us to connect with people around the world. Facebook, Twitter, Instagram and other platforms help us keep up to date with significant landmarks in the lives of all our connections: weddings, birthdays, new jobs – and frequently what they are having for dinner. We form WhatsApp groups of old school friends. We wish estranged family members Happy Birthday. These small online interactions are to our friendships what a pilot light is to a gas boiler; they keep the flame of connection alight in between our physical meetings. But a pilot light is no good for cooking anything meaningful.

And yet, with regard to friendship, screens have a worryingly detrimental effect, and this should regularly cause us to monitor the amount of time their pixels hold our gaze. In this section we are going to focus on just one of the aspects – how these high-definition televisions, tablets and telephones take our *time* hostage.

One of my favourite pre-Christmas activities is delivering cards around our neighbourhood. As a church we print a card for every home to wish them a Happy Christmas and invite them to the various services. For most of my life, the early weekends in December have been spent rushing up and down hundreds of driveways, opening and closing gates, and trying to survive without losing a finger as my hands push the cards through letterboxes with dogs on the other side. Often, the houses have living rooms that look out on to the garden path and I get a small glimpse into the lives of those in my community through the net curtains. There is almost always a television on.

Along the timeline of human history, there has never been a period when there has been a stronger attraction to sit at home and be enthralled by the wealth of entertainment available at the touch of a button, or now by voice-activated control. Time that we used to spend with others, in pubs, social clubs, churches or other third spaces, is now spent in front of box-sets. I'm with Jon Yates when he says, 'It is hard to overstate the extent to which the invention of TV and now streaming has changed how we use our leisure time.'[12] The average UK adult spends three-and-a-half hours watching television each day, amounting to 78,705 hours, 3,639 movies and 31,507 episodes over their lifetime.[13] Netflix identifies its main rival not as another streaming service. In the war for our attention, it is targeting our time: 'Sleep is our competition.'[14]

That's before we consider how much time we spend scrolling through photos, videos and statuses on social media platforms, the algorithms working overtime, fighting tooth and (thumb)nail to provide personalized content to keep our eyes glued to the screen. It all adds up. I get a terrifying notification telling me each Monday morning just how much I've been staring at amusing trivia and clips of 1990s sporting moments. Younger generations are particularly susceptible, spending a third of their entire leisure time on devices.[15]

At its best, technology is a gift to friendship. At its worst, the devices designed to connect us end up doing the opposite. Combined with the ever-improving experience of home entertainment, and jobs that demand more and more from us, if time is the oxygen of friendship, we are gasping for breath.

As Jack Bauer would say, we don't have much time. Invest it wisely. Invest it in friendship.

Fakebook

The pressure that social media places on our relationships goes beyond the battle for our time and is worthy of some discussion here. First, consider what it could do to our perception of friendship. I still remember the rush of my first few hours on Facebook as the friend requests streamed in. I had just finished university and started work. My network was sizeable. Within hours my Facebook connections were into triple figures, and I was friends with a guy

I once played football with, a girl I sat next to in lectures, my sister, and a boy I went to school with whom I vaguely remember once eating a crayon. Fifteen years on, I'd struggle to recognize many of my 'friends'.

I love social media – more because I love people than I love the dopamine rush that arrives when I have a notification that someone has 'liked' something I've posted. But it is not always a friend of friendship. Becoming friends with someone on your social media platform is almost effortless. Clicking on the 'Accept' button requires no commitment from us, and yet when the transaction is complete, we feel that our friendship circle has widened. Social media can be dangerous when it creates the illusion of friendship and deceives us into thinking we have a quantity or quality of relationship that is misrepresentative of reality.

Sociologist Sherry Turkle describes it like this: 'Digital connections and the sociable robot may offer the *illusion of companionship* without the demands of friendship' (emphasis added)[16] Friendship is demanding and costly, and requires us to become vulnerable and be hurt. There is nothing wrong with making friends online, as long as we do so in real life as well. Social media at its best is a tool and technology that enhances rather than replaces in-person, physical relationships.

Second, let's consider what these media do to our perception of ourselves. Our own self-esteem, self-consciousness and self-awareness play an important role in our ability to relate well to others. A common experience of many is that the world of social media platforms has a harmful effect on how we feel about ourselves. A 2017 study found that social media was the most frequently cited answer when 11 to 18s were asked: who/what are the top three people/things that make you feel bad about yourself.[17] Research from The Prince's Trust discovered that 46% of 16- to 25-year-olds say that comparing themselves to others on social media makes them feel inadequate.[18] As a teenager I was fairly confident, but had an army of insecurities that would occasionally come marauding into my unguarded and susceptible psyche. I am glad social media arrived too late to reinforce their attacks.

The challenge for all of us is that this impact on our self-perception affects not only us. It impacts our relationships with others. Our online personas act as an extension of ourselves and the temptation to curate, filter and enhance how people see us online can be irresistible. If we then fall into the trap of comparison, we end up comparing our real selves to the aspirational, filtered version of our friends that they have projected online. The effect is observed by author Jonah Lynch:

> Take Facebook profile photos: most don't necessarily reflect what a person really is, but rather what he or she would like to seem. It is a small and absolutely pardonable vanity, but unveils a way of being that eats away at friendship.[19]

Third, we must acknowledge that as well as enhancing our connection with others, technology can have an extremely detrimental effect on friendship if used badly. Sometimes the medium we use to communicate with can create or compound conflict with our connections. On one hand, the communication tools we have at our disposal are indisputably of great help in maintaining and strengthening friendships. There are a multitude of occasions when a text message, an email or even an emoji is a suitable medium for communication with a contact. But I would wager there are a greater number of relationships that have been damaged or discontinued because one party chose an unwise medium to communicate what they had to say. One in four of us have said something online that we later regretted and would never have said in a face-to-face conversation.[20] A 2014 Voucher Cloud survey found that a whopping 56% of people who had ended a relationship had done so digitally, 25% via text message.[21]

The digital revolution has led to more available information than our forefathers could have dreamed of. Sadly, information is not the same as wisdom. When it comes to friendship, it is the latter that we so desperately need if technology is to fulfil its promise to enhance our relationships rather than expose their vulnerabilities.

The flesh

When it comes to the quality of our friendships, we can so often be our own worst enemies. Our first problem is our own selfishness. Even after we have become Christians our selfishness and sinfulness can be a huge barrier in forming meaningful friendships. As we will discover in the chapters ahead, sacrifice, hospitality and vulnerability are not just side orders at the table of friendship but rather the main course in our staple relational diet.

If you are anything like me, you will have much to repent of in this area, much to reflect on with regret. With great shame I remember one occasion when I abandoned a school friend to be accepted by the in-crowd. There have been many times over the years when requests have arrived for help or companionship and I have rejected them – not in a spirit of wisdom and wanting to maintain healthy boundaries, but in one of self-centredness, because I have been greedy with my own time and company.

Pastor and author Paul Tripp describes sin as 'fundamentally anti-social, because sin causes me to love me more than anything else and to care for me more than anything else'.[22] Our motives for friendship are important. Relationships that begin on a dishonest, disingenuous or selfish basis are often destined for disaster and disappointment.

I remember one time the alarm went off painfully early. I clumsily knocked it off the bedside table before turning it off, prompting a grunt of disapproval from my wife.

'How can sleep be over already?' I grumbled in a whisper as I tip-toed downstairs to the clothes I had set out the night before in an effort not to wake the whole family selecting my outfit from the creaky wardrobe. After a glass of water, the adrenaline kicked in with the memory that I was up early to speak at an exciting event. I hurriedly put on my best suit, glanced approvingly in the mirror, sprayed myself with my best aftershave, ensured my bag was packed and picked up my phone from the charger before heading to the car. I blinked at the screen on my device as it lit up. Why was the time wrong? 'Oh *no*!' I groaned in horror as I realized what had happened. My alarm had been set to the wrong time. It was still the middle of the night.

A relationship based just on what I can get out of it is like a day that unintentionally begins in the middle of the night. Its footing is unsound and it is unlikely to last the course.

The tension we all experience is that we enter into and live in relationship as both image bearers of the relational God, but also broken, fragile individuals who are susceptible to sinful and selfish motives and behaviour. Being aware and honest about this aspect of the pressure on our friendships can help us to uncover, name and fight it. Like the moment in the plot of a drama when the undercover agent is unmasked, the power sin has over us and our friendships is broken when we expose it and deal with it before God. It is important to recognize the adversary within.

But we aren't our worst enemies. There's also the enemy 'without'.

The devil

The devil's goal is to first isolate us.[23]
(John Mark Comer)

Have you ever felt that life is a battle? That our relationships especially are more hard work than they ought to be? Part of the reason we feel this is that there is a very real enemy who opposes us and what is good for us. When we think about a force of evil in the world, the first images that spring to mind can be a fiery Hollywood demon 'hell-bent' on violence and destruction, or a cartoon devil whispering temptation into a listening ear.

The Bible in general, and Jesus in particular, is clear that there is one who stands in the way of us thriving, spiritually and relationally. Jesus called him Satan, which literally means 'opposer' or 'adversary', and he is not a fan of our relationships prospering.

Satan hates friendship. Where God's heart is for unity and relational human flourishing in the church and society, Satan's is for division and destruction. There is a fascinating moment that demonstrates this in 2 Corinthians. Paul is writing to encourage the church there to forgive someone who has hurt them deeply: 'Now instead, you ought to forgive and comfort him, so that he will not be overwhelmed by excessive sorrow. I urge you, therefore, to reaffirm your love for him' (2 Corinthians 2:7–8). The final reason given for this outpouring of love is startling: 'in order that Satan might not outwit us. For we are not unaware of his schemes' (v. 11). In that knowing way in which someone communicates when they feel they have the measure of an opponent and have out-thought and out-guessed them, Paul sees through the 'schemes' of the devil and urges the church not to be outwitted by him in the relational arena. Don't let him get in and divide you.

In another instance, when writing to the Ephesian church, in a section of the letter all about relationships, Paul links inauthenticity, dishonesty and resentment in relationship to giving the devil leverage in our lives and our friendships:

Therefore each of you must put off falsehood and speak truth-fully to your neighbour, for we are all members of one body. 'In your anger do not sin': do not let the sun go down while you are still angry, and do not give the devil a foothold.
(Ephesians 4:25–27)

I have been part of some extraordinary teams over the years. Often, especially at critical moments, there is an uncanny, common feeling that an external force is seeking to create friction and division in relationships. As I have spoken to others, they have recognized the same effect. I am sure it is not always the case, but I am equally certain that sometimes it is; that the external agent is the enemy seeking to divide and destroy unity in teams and integrity in friendship. Satan is seeking to drive wedges between friends.

But what is the nature of this pressure? How does he go about his work? Jesus referred to him as 'a liar and the father of lies' (John 8:44). Truth and trust are the bricks and mortar that build a friendship. Lies and deceit act like wrecking balls and sledgehammers to its structure. When it comes to relationships, the enemy may seek to lie to us to undermine our status towards each other.

If he can get us to believe that we are too good, or not good enough, to be friends with the other, the wall may take a hammer blow. If he can incite jealousy and envy and cause us to resent rather than celebrate the successes of a friend, the structure may take another knock. If he can persuade us that we are the only ones making the effort, that a friendship has become one sided and our needs aren't being met while the other party is always getting his or her own way, the walls may begin to tumble. If he can expose all our insecurities, remind us of past relational breakdowns, provoke us to keep our defences up, distort our thinking into believing we either don't need friends or that no-one would possibly want to spend time with us, our relationships may be left in ruins.

But we are not unaware of his schemes.

We began this chapter by highlighting the importance of understanding the pressure on our friendships. If making friends and maintaining relationships is difficult for you, I hope you feel encouraged that at least you now know why. Internal and external forces press us from every direction. Our ability to live in friendship in its fullness is squeezed and squashed by the cultural conditions we find ourselves in, undermined from within by our own fleshly flaws, and at war with an enemy that seeks its destruction.

Suffocated from the outside, sabotaged from within and occasionally under attack, is it really possible for our relationships to thrive? Can we harness the sheer power of this God-given gift and live in its blessing against the odds? Is it possible to be the best of friends?

The themes of this chapter can be explored further using small-group resources, videos and discussion questions. Delve deeper at: www.philknox.co.uk

Further reading

N. Carr, *The Shallows* (W. W. Norton, New York, 2010). If you want to know what using the internet does to your brain, Carr examines the science of the effects of our online activities on our brain.

J. M. Comer, *Live No Lies* (Form, London, 2021). A masterful call to arms against the enemies of disciples of Jesus in today's cultural waters.

J. Rice, *The Church of Facebook* (Colorado Springs CO, David C. Cook, 2009). An important, pioneering book in the early years of social media, many of the themes are still relevant.

3

Circles of friends

If you have two friends in your lifetime, you're lucky. If you have one good friend, you're more than lucky.
(S. E. Hinton, *That Was Then, This Is Now*)

What is a friend? The word 'friend' describes a vast range of human connection. My wife Dani and I are on more than good terms and yet she is also my friend. The other day as I was getting out of a taxi, the driver said, 'Have a good day, my friend.' Last week I met someone at a meeting; we are now friends online. I met Jon on our first day of school in 1988 and we hang out roughly every other weekend. I grab a catch-up curry with Callum about once a year. I met Oli on holiday over ten years ago and I've not seen him in person since. I sit next to Rich at work. As I describe these relationships, I am aware that they embody a lengthy spectrum of intimacy and frequency of contact and emotional connection. Life, for all of us, is a rich, complex and tangled tapestry of friendships. The picture is made up of old friends, school friends, family friends, church friends, more-than-just-friends, work mates, teammates, best mates, pub mates, spouses and taxi drivers.

Here is the bad news of this book: you cannot be friends with everyone.

Here is the good news of this book: you cannot be friends with everyone.

I have two sons. They are six years apart in age. Occasionally someone asks me for some advice on being a dad. I usually respond, 'Whatever you do, don't think you have got the parenting thing sorted after the first child.' Despite the age gap, Caleb and Jos are so different in character and interests. Nevertheless, as their father, I am determined that they know I love them both in equal measure. I try to balance my words of praise, time spent with each and amount spent on them at birthdays.

Friendship is not the same.

You do not have to treat all your friends the same. The taxi driver will not be getting expensive jewellery for Christmas.

It is a good thing to have different grades, levels and depths of friendship. C. S. Lewis writes of the merits of investing in some more than others: 'We do not disparage silver by distinguishing it from gold.'[1] It is understandable and easy to feel that we need to treat our friends with equality comparable to the equality I give to my sons. The reality is that we have limited time, bandwidth and emotional energy. The temptation in our excess-ridden world is to take on more and more relationships far beyond our saturation point. The consequence of doing so is that we can unwittingly disperse our finite relational capacity so thinly that, in C. S. Lewis's terms, we have plenty of silver but no gold. We all need golden friendships. As H. Black says: 'The commonest mistake is that we spread our intercourse over a mass and have no depth of heart left. We lament that we have no staunch and faithful friend when we have not expended the love which produces such.'[2]

When it comes to friendship, quantity is no substitute for quality.

Making friends on purpose

Much of what my 9-year-old son Caleb watches online makes me want to take a sledgehammer to the internet (Exhibit A: 'Raining Tacos' – don't search for it as you will instantly regret the assault on your senses). However, there are a couple of types of video that make my eyes linger and provide a momentary distraction. One of these is trick-shot videos, which are responsible for billions of views, likes and shares (mostly from my son). I have seen people do things with darts, table-tennis balls and paper aeroplanes I scarcely thought possible. Part of the art of the trick shot is to make it appear as though it has happened by accident and at the first attempt. Inevitably when Caleb tries to recreate these moments in our home, success is rare, and he wonders why it doesn't work out quite the same as online.

Friendship does not happen by accident. Friendship is a choice.

Like a trick-shot video, some people make it look effortless, and our attempts can feel like Caleb's amateur recreations, but great friendship takes a great deal of time and intentionality. And that means choosing how we spend our time, who we spend it with and who we don't spend it with. Those decisions are not easy. But they are necessary if we are to be purposeful friends rather than just let friendship happen to us. If we are not intentional, we risk an abundance of silver at the expense of a poverty of gold.

Choosing our friends wisely is necessary if we are to be the best of friends.

Furthermore, choosing to become friends with someone is a costly choice. To choose to enter a relationship where you are dependent on someone else and they depend on you is to curtail and restrict some of your independent choices. Professor William K. Rawlins identifies these opposing forces of independence and dependence in friendship. Both are important: 'Complete independence means no relationship at all, and total dependence constrains both persons by subverting their individual integrity. The ongoing mutual enactment of some composite of these freedoms is essential to maintain a bond of friendship.'[3]

To choose to be a friend is to deny yourself some of your autonomy. The degree of intimacy in the relationship will drastically affect the amount of freedom you are sacrificing. At one end of the spectrum, the cost of my 'friendship' with the taxi driver is so small as to be not worth giving thought to. At the other end, I promised Dani in 2008 that I would share everything, forsaking all others, till death do us part. That one has been quite expensive. Each of my other relationships falls somewhere in between those two.

Every friendship contains this dance, this trade-off, where I sacrifice something of myself and lay down part of my life for another. In this chapter we explore how to choose how much we give of ourselves to different grades and depths of relationship. Will you come with me to discover the gold? Because I believe that God has given us the wisdom we need to be friends on purpose. I believe it is both woven into creation and revealed in the life of Jesus.

Friendship circles

A friend of mine says that good science just tells us what God already knew. In the coming pages we are going to explore the most recent academic findings regarding the various levels of intimacy we are created to have capacity for. We will then map that on to the way Jesus intentionally structured his own relationships and discover a remarkable correlation. Let me begin by introducing you to my guide through the research in this area: anthropologist and psychologist Robin Dunbar.

Pythagoras had a triangle, Pavlov had a dog and Dunbar has a number. That number is 150.

Robin Dunbar's premise is that 150 is the limit to the number of relationships we can realistically sustain, based on the size of our brains. They are not your social media contacts, or the people you would smile at in the street. These are the people in our lives whom we would not feel embarrassed about joining uninvited for a drink if we happened to bump into them in a bar.[4] We would feel comfortable joining them for a train journey if we saw them unexpectedly on the same platform. 'They would immediately know who you are and where you stand in relation to them, and you would know where they stand in relation to you. Your relationship has a history. No introductions needed.'[5]

We have physical and emotional limitations when it comes to the number of friends we can have. Our brains cannot cope with thousands of meaningful connections, let alone our diaries. We are fearfully and wonderfully made; relationally wired but with finite capacity.

Dunbar goes further to suggest that there are layers to reflect the strengths of various friendships above and below his 150. While we can have meaningful friendship with many, we can only have an intimate connection with a few. He breaks the numbers down as follows:

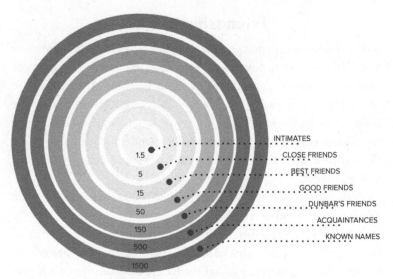

Figure 1 **Dunbar's friends**

1.5 – Intimates Many people have a best friend and/or a spouse whom they would describe as their closest friendship. His argument for the number being 1.5 is that there are some who have a best friend *and* a spouse, so this averages out as a half. I have yet to meet anyone with half a friend.

5 – Close friends This is the next layer, which comprises those we feel emotionally very close to and typically contact at least once a week. Known as 'the support clique', this group contains the shoulders to cry on when life falls apart.

15 – Best friends As your social circles extend, these are the friends you will typically see at least once a month. There are still strong feelings of emotional attachment, and from this group come those you will regularly choose to hang out with in social settings.

50 - Good friends Imagine you are throwing a significant birthday party. This is the guest list. They are those you might greet with a warm physical welcome and smile but might not share your most pressing problems with. (I know hugs aren't for everyone, so perhaps a hearty handshake or fist bump.)

150 – Dunbar's friends You would not hesitate to go over and sit next to them if you happened to see them at 3 a.m. in Hong Kong airport.[6] They are on your Christmas card list (if you send them). You probably have contact with them approximately once or twice a year.

500 – Acquaintances You are friends with this group on your social media platform. You know who they are, but you probably wouldn't go to their wedding or funeral. You may have had closer ties at one stage, but the sands of time have worn away at the bonds that brought you together.

1,500 – Known names Dunbar speculates that there are about this many faces we can put names to. Clearly not all of these people will know who we are; most of us will recognize the profile on a postage stamp but would not be on talking terms with His Majesty.

As I have explored the work of Robin Dunbar, I have heard a relentless voice calling me towards comparing the most up-to-date scientific analysis with the ancient wisdom of the relational God. And as I have done so I have discovered that there are astonishing similarities. It turns out that even Jesus felt the need to think about how he invested his time and energies into relationships of varying strengths. It turns out the theories of the latest and greatest brains of today reflect the life of the man who claimed to be friendship's founder.

Jesus: our masterclass

Even though the gold-laden Mr T from *The A-Team* is a hero of mine, I've never worn very much jewellery. It took me at least a couple of months to get used to my wedding ring. But as a teenager, the one piece I wore was a bracelet with the inscription 'WWJD?'. It was a great conversation starter with friends. Many speculated what it might mean before I explained, occasionally with great pride and sometimes with a degree of embarrassment: 'What would Jesus do?' I didn't have much street cred to play with anyway, so the negative impact on this was negligible, but I do believe that at times this simple acronym inspired me to consider my behaviour and occasionally helped me act in a more Christlike way.

If you had asked me back then, however, what it meant to do what Jesus would do, I would probably have simplified my response to not doing bad stuff and being nice to people. Now that's not a bad start when it comes to following Jesus, but as Christians, as 'little Christs', he is our example in everything, and we seldom consider his example in relationships. If we do go this far, we are likely only to talk about his 'how to relate to' rather than his 'who to relate to'. But his pattern of relationships is a masterclass and model. So, when it came to choosing companions, what *did* Jesus do?

First, Jesus actually had friends. This was an important lens through which he regarded his connection with his disciples. This in itself would have been astonishing to some of his contemporaries. There is no evidence anywhere else of other rabbis regarding their disciples in this way.[7] Jesus broke the rules and social barriers with the scandalous and disarming statement 'I have called you friends' (John 15:15). It was not the primary way in which he understood his relationship with them, but is significant nonetheless.

Second, Jesus was purposeful about his relationships. He didn't just let them happen to him; he was wise, considered and even strategic in choosing his friends, explicitly saying to his closest disciples, 'You did not choose me, but I chose you' (John 15:16). The context here is important. Jesus was their rabbi. The practice in the first century for disciples searching for a teacher was that they would approach the teacher with a request to become his apprentice. Jesus reversed this recruitment practice. He actively sought out his followers and chose them.

Third, Jesus was prayerful. Luke deliberately details the decision-making process of Jesus in choosing his apostles. He went to a mountain to pray for a whole night and then gathered his team (Luke 6:12). Many of us will not have spent even a minute praying about who we should surround ourselves with, let alone a whole night.

Fourth, Jesus formed circles of friends. This is an idea that can be troubling to grapple with: the Son of God did not treat people equally. There were some people with whom he deliberately spent more time than others. It is uncomfortable to consider that by choosing some he excluded others. His embracing of human likeness and personhood meant that he had the same limitations we all face in terms of relational bandwidth and capacity for connectivity. Everyone mattered to Jesus, but that did not mean everyone got the same amount of him. So, what did his circles look like?

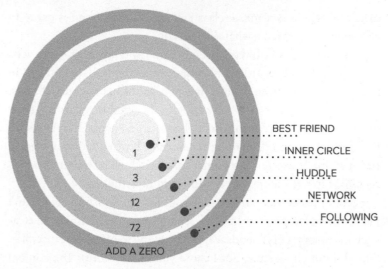

Figure 2 **Jesus' friends**

One – Jesus had a best friend John was 'the disciple whom Jesus loved' (John 13:23). With this friend, Jesus seems to have shared more of his life and allowed him greater access to his heart and teaching.

Three – Jesus had an inner circle Peter, James and John were the disciples the Son of God spent the most time with. They were invited to be present at some of the highest and lowest moments of his ministry, and to accompany him on significant journeys.

Twelve – Jesus had a huddle This is the circle of friends we are most familiar with. They were not all afforded the same time and opportunity as the inner circle, but appear repeatedly through the gospels in Jesus' company, care and confidence. It seems that Jesus had a meaningful relationship with each of them.

Seventy-two – Jesus had a network It is clear that beyond the Twelve there were others with whom Christ had varying degrees of regular contact and intimacy. Luke describes the commissioning of seventy-two of these; mention is also given to Mary, Martha and Lazarus (John 11), Joanna and Susanna (Luke 8). There were undoubtedly more in this category. This circle were Jesus' Christmas card list and if the departure lounge at Hong Kong airport had existed . . .

Add a zero – Jesus had a following There were lots of people who met him only once or twice: guests at parties, fellow travellers on the way to Galilee, Legion, the unnamed woman at the well. It's almost certain that many of these would have wanted to stay in touch, but they remained acquaintances, kept at arm's length by situation or intention.

I hope that as I have described Jesus' circles of friends, you have noticed not only the fact that he decided to structure his relational connections in the first place, but also the striking similarities with Dunbar's numbers. It's as if he had inside knowledge of the needs and nature of human friendship. It's as if he had privileged access to the hardwiring of humanity that science would reveal thousands of years later. It's as if he were more than just a man . . .

I want to urge you to be more Christlike in your friendships. By that I do mean in your character and the way you relate to them. But I also mean in the way you think about the architecture of your circles and the various levels of intimacy you strive for with the range of people in your life. I want to encourage you to learn from Jesus' purposeful nature, to lean on his example of prayerful consideration and to be intentional in creating circles of connections around you. Applying these three principles will allow your relationships to flourish, no matter what the size, scale or strength of your existing circles.

And at the heart of your relational world, today's sociologists and the God of eternity seem to agree: you need one person with whom to build the strongest of bonds.

Further reading

R. Dunbar, *Friends* (Little, Brown, London, 2021). This is the outstanding work referred to throughout this book, exploring the anthropology of friendship from a variety of angles.

P. Parker, *The Art of Gathering* (Penguin, London, 2018). Among insights into meetings of all sizes, if you want to run a conference, throw a party or host a family gathering, Priya Parker will help you think about the journey from start to finish.

4

One – Jesus had a best friend

Life is an awful, ugly place to not have a best friend.
(Sarah Dessen, *Someone Like You*)

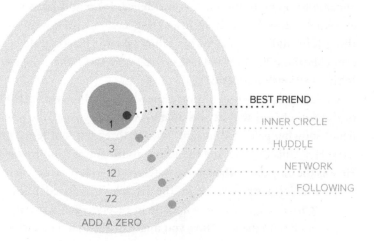

Occasionally friendship is as simple as who you sit next to.

Mark Rigby was my first best friend. Our friendship began in Mrs Andrews' class. We shared a passion for football, talking at the back of class and competing against one another in almost every school subject. In whatever environment we found ourselves we just wanted to be next to each other. In the classroom, the only way to stop us talking was to separate us and sit us next to girls, whom we considered repulsive (we were 6 years old). In the playground, it was unthinkable that we would play on the opposite team to one another – to do so would be to sever a strike partnership that was, in our minds, up there with the most legendary in world football. When it comes to best friends, proximity matters.

Who did Jesus sit next to?

Leonardo da Vinci's depiction of the Last Supper surpasses even the playground football prowess of Mark and me in terms of its iconic nature. It is unlikely that Jesus and the apostles sat as depicted, all on one side of the table, and the exact seating plan is not described in the Bible, but one thing we do know is that reclining next to Jesus was John (John 13:23). Upon further inspection, this adjacency appears to be more than just coincidence. John and Jesus had an extremely close bond. It seems sitting next to Jesus was something John did so regularly, his mum asked if he could do so for ever (Matthew 20:21). What else do we know about the closeness of John's relationship to Jesus?

First, John had such an intimate knowledge of the events in the life of the Son of God that he was able to write his gospel, the level of detail showing profound insight into the three years of Jesus' ministry. His vantage point was the most prominent of front-row seats. He was the only one of the Twelve watching on as Jesus was crucified.

Second, John is referred to as 'the disciple Jesus loved' five times in this gospel. He is the only apostle to receive such a prestigious title – albeit self-labelled. Now, you might argue that if you were the author of a book about Jesus, you might like to describe yourself in such terms, but John would have known that his account would be read by others in the inner circles and his claim subject to scrutiny. At the Last Supper, it was John whom Jesus confided in (John 13:26). At the cross, it was John he entrusted his mother to (John 19:26–27). Few could claim a closer emotional connection to him during his earthly ministry and this relationship was intentional on Jesus' part. He chose who he sat next to.

But what does 'best' friendship look like and how do we even begin to find one?

Making friends

Some people are natural friend-makers. Watching someone like this in action can be like watching a master craftsman at work. I have seen people walk into rooms where they know nobody and within minutes strangers are interacting with them as if they have known each other for decades. By the end of the conversation there are hugs and exchanges of contact details, and the rest of us are left watching on with as much exasperation as admiration, thinking, 'They make it look so easy!'

Most of us do not possess the friend-maker superpower. But we are all made in the image of the relational God and friendship is his gift to us. Whatever our personality type, however we are wired, whatever the hurts and betrayals of the past, we can all make friends. Friendship is the sandpit in which we all get to play. Perhaps, as you read this, you find yourself in a new environment needing to make new connections. Perhaps you have never experienced the type of deep, life-giving friendship you yearn for. Perhaps the pandemic or other recent events have changed the fabric of your relational networks and you find yourself at a moment where your connections need rebooting or re-kindling. Unless making friends is your superpower, the chances are you, like me, could benefit from understanding how friends are made.

The great Connector

The journalist and author Malcolm Gladwell describes a nuanced version of the type of people who have friend-making superpowers. They are those who have not only lots of connections, but also a particular gift and tendency to make introductions that catalyse others to connect. They don't just make friends with people; they make people make friends. They are a walking, talking speed-dating service. Gladwell describes them as 'people with a special gift for bringing the world together'.[1]

Think about your own network of friends and how you first met them. There will likely be a variety of different ways and settings in which these relationships first started. And it is also likely that there are a few friends whom you met through the same person. My friend Andy, for example, is a connector. There are at least ten people I know because Andy introduced us. 'Connectors know lots of people. They are the kinds of people who know everyone. All of us know someone like this. But I don't think we spend a lot of time thinking about the importance of these kinds of people.'[2]

It is worthwhile identifying the connectors in your life. When you become friends with someone through social media, you are not surprised to see connectors as mutual friends. When it comes to making friends, these individuals are a helpful catalyst.

But there is a greater Connector who is under-consulted in the friend-making process.

God is the great Friend-maker. His creative work since the dawn of time has been to create not isolated individuals but communities of interconnected humans. He still believes it is not good for men and women to be alone, and loves bringing people together. I believe it is a great source of joy to the heart of the Father when two of his children meet and the electric connection of friendship begins to spark. I picture him saying to the angels, 'Look at those two! I knew they would get along.' A beautiful example of God's commitment to this is found when Jesus, while in agony on the cross, asks John to look after his mother and his mother to look after John (John 19:26–27). Even during this cataclysmic moment in history, God is making connections and uniting a family.

In prayer, we can invite the great Connector to help us in this area. Don't just pray for the friends you have made; pray for the making of friends. A wonderful prayer you can pray for others is that God would provide great people to surround them. I pray that prayer regularly for my children. I know that their lives depend on the people God will place in their lives. Jonathan Holmes, when asked where to begin in the process of forging friendship, said, 'Pray! I find this to be an underestimated step. Ask God to prepare you for biblical friendship, and then for wisdom in whom to pursue.'[3]

Friendship is more of an art than a formula. As we explore these steps on the common pathways to making friends, they are not as simple as punching the numbers into one side of a mathematical equation, knowing the answer is a perfect relationship on the other side. But they are well-worn, biblical and prudent principles that will help you on the relational journey.

Under our noses

In C. S. Lewis's *The Silver Chair*, Jill and Edmund are searching for a ruined city to find a lost prince. Aslan has told them that the city bears instructions for the next stage in their quest. Unwittingly, they stumble into the city they are searching for, but a snowstorm prevents them from realizing that is where they are. Only upon looking back on the journey they have taken do they realize not only that they walked right through the very place they were looking for, but that the streets formed the instructions for the next leg of their adventure. The answer was right under their noses, but they missed it.

Sometimes we miss the people God is providing for us because we do not look well enough at those he has put right in front of us. I love the way Jesus noticed people. His eyes searched for divine activity for him to join in with: 'the Son can . . . do only what he sees the Father doing' (John 5:19). He saw the crippled woman and called her forward (Luke 13:12). He noticed Zacchaeus in the sycamore tree (Luke 19:5). I get the impression that his eyes regularly scanned the scenery, looking at the people placed in his path.

When it came to choosing his disciples, the gospel writers are deliberate in describing Jesus' first interactions with his closest friends. 'As Jesus walked beside the Sea of Galilee, he *saw* Simon and his brother Andrew casting a net into the lake' (Mark 1:16, emphasis added). He first cast eyes on the disciple he loved three verses later: 'When he had gone a little farther, he *saw* James son of Zebedee and his brother John in a boat' (Mark 1:19, emphasis added). I don't believe in love at first sight, but I do believe that love begins with looking. Don't miss the people God brings into your eyeline. Sometimes the friendship we need is right in front of us.

'You too'

As we will discover in the chapters ahead, there is great virtue and merit in being friends with people who are different from you, but most friendships, and especially 'best' friendships, are built on the foundations of having significant things in common.

My best friend is called Adam. If our friendship were a house, the architect first put pencil to paper in 1996, when we began to get the same bus to school together. The foundations were laid when we discovered we found the same things, and each other, funny. Hours of laughter put the groundwork in place alongside common interests in football, fitness and computer games. There were important differences as well. Adam and I had completely different upbringings and family lives, but there was an unquestionable chemistry that remains to this day. The house of our friendship has had many extensions and storeys (and stories) added in that time, but I still recognize the foundational structures. Twenty-five years on I still laugh more with him than any other person, we still watch a lot of football in each other's company and regularly weight train and run together.

When making friends, finding reciprocal interests, perspectives and experiences is inescapable. We are wired to mine for likeness. The house of friendship is built on common ground. C. S. Lewis describes the birth of friendship like this:

Friendship arises out of mere Companionship when two or more of the companions discover they have in common some insight or interest or even taste which the others do not share and which, till that moment, each believed to be his own unique treasure (or burden). The typical expression of opening Friendship would be something like, 'What? You too? I thought I was the only one.'[4]

This observation then begs the questions: what kind of things might I have in common with potential friends? What are the common foundations for friendships? These are helpful questions to ask of the friends you already have or have had. But what does the research in this area tell us? For this we defer once more to our guide Robin Dunbar. He describes seven 'pillars' of friendship that he found were the most common factors to be shared by the best of friends:

- Speaking the same language
- Growing up in the same place
- Having the same education and occupation
- Holding the same worldview
- Sharing the same hobbies and interests
- Finding the same things funny
- Listening to the same music.[5]

When building a relationship, the more of these pillars holding up the first floor, the greater the chance the house will stand. When you are searching for the best of friends this is a useful starting point. With Jesus and John, we can easily tick off a few on the list: they spoke the same language and grew up in the same place. They were probably educated to a similar level, entering a family trade at a young age, but they did not share the same work and I am curious as to why Jesus chose fishermen rather than fellow carpenters. Next, the question of worldview is interesting to consider. It's clear that after three years in each other's company John's worldview had been transformed into a kingdom mindset, but we must also presume that Jesus chose him either because he shared some of these values to begin with or because he possessed a teachability and malleability that the Son of God knew he could work with. With regard to the rest, we sadly don't know. I wish we had greater insight into their relationship. I love to imagine Jesus laughing with his friends and comparing notes on the latest lyre player on the Judean music scene. I suspect he was quite good at card games.

From good to great to best

Most of us will have experienced the journey I have described so far. We meet another, there is a connection over common interests, but we are not quite at the stage where we would offer them one of our kidneys. What happens next?

Some friendships catch like wildfire. There is a seemingly instant click, an exchange of phone numbers, and before you know it you are swapping secrets and laughing emojis, and you feel as though you have known that person far longer than the twenty-four hours since you first shook hands. Others are slow burners – they initially grow much more slowly. Best friendships develop in different ways. Just because, to mix the metaphors in this chapter, you don't get on like a house on fire in the first hour of connection it might not mean that a deep friendship cannot be established. Equally, just because there is an initial blaze it doesn't mean there will be a lifelong relationship. The next stages are critical.

A colleague says that when developing a friendship, it is the 'second coffee' that is the most important. Most people you connect with will agree to meet for the first time, but it is the subsequent meeting that begins to solidify things and kindle the fragile flame. Jonathan Holmes agrees: 'Consistency of pursuit will be crucial to forming friendships. Too often, people begin with energy and good intentions, but then let things fall by the wayside.'[6] Friends are found, but they are also made, and we move on now to consider three critical ingredients in their making.

1 Time

We return to that finite yet fundamental factor. When we consider Jesus' strategy of influence on the world, it is easy to overlook that a core component of his game plan was to simply spend time with people. So much time, we have four detailed accounts of his teaching and ministry. Have you ever stopped to think that if Jesus had gone solo, he may have got a lot more done, but would have failed to leave the legacy of the men and women who launched the planet's most successful start-up and the human authors of the world's best-selling book of all time? One of Jesus' greatest investments was time, in people like John. Mark writes of his purpose in recruiting the apostles, 'that they might be *with* him' (Mark 3:14, emphasis added). He surrounded himself with men he would go on to call his friends.

I have done some stupid things for charity over the years. I once ran a half-marathon in green body paint as the Incredible Hulk. I have endured gales, downpours, hills, sunburn, ice baths and Lycra cycling from Land's End to John o' Groats. I even helped break a world record for the longest ever five-a-side football match (I was on the losing team – after forty-eight hours we lost by over 300 goals, and my knees have never quite been the same). But equally as memorable as those exploits is a challenge I took on with a friend of mine called Barry. Not content with climbing the tallest mountains in Wales, England and Scotland in the space of twenty-four hours, Barry convinced me that people would donate much more money if we added four more mountains over the following four days – a venture he christened 'The Seven Deadlies'.

The next week of my life was glorious, torturous and everything in between. My eyes spent some of it wide open at the most stunning sunrises and sunsets from rough and rocky ridges. At times they squinted as hail battered my grimaced face, rain poured from my forehead and the wind battered relentlessly against our forward progress. But for much of the week, as we walked in formation on mountain paths, all I could see was Barry. When I opened them in the morning the first thing I saw was Barry. As he turned the light off ahead of a night of far too little sleep in a hostel, his was the last form I saw. Each waking hour, we ate, climbed, scrambled or drove together in a car that smelled so bad by the last mountain I gag at the thought of it.

I am not sure I have ever spent as long, with such little sleep, in someone's company like that. The result was that an existing relationship was pushed to warp speed during a short space of time. We now share not only the memories from days that exceeded 60,000 steps and punished my knees already scarred from two days and nights of football, but another level of depth to our friendship. That's what time does. When you think of similar examples of intense amounts of time spent sharing a common experience in the presence of another, I suspect you will observe a similar impact.

Good friendships take time, great friendships take a long time and the best take even longer. But do we know how long? That was the question asked by Professor Jeffrey A. Hall in a 2019 study.[7] He wanted to know how long it took for acquaintances to become best friends. He surveyed 355 adults who had relocated and begun to form new friendships. They were asked about the friends they had made and their emotional closeness and commitment to them. They were then asked about the amount of time they had spent with them over nine weeks and how that time was spent.

This is what he found:

Casual friends These are the ones who may well make your Christmas card list and may just about get to your wedding. To form this kind of friendship takes about thirty hours of contact time.

Friends We move up a layer through the spheres of intimacy. These friends are in the middle ground between a wave in the street and a bearhug. In Jesus' circles, these formed the network. Hall found that these friendships emerged after fifty hours of time spent together.

Good friends Intensity of relationship is increasing and so is the cost to our busy schedules. With friends like these we share strong emotional connections. This is the Twelve in Jesus' world. Hall's research found that these bonds do not appear until over 140 hours have been spent together.

Best friends So how long does it take to trust someone to let them into your inner circle? At the centre of Jesus' relationships, this probably equates to the level of intimacy he had with John, Peter and James. These friends only emerge after 300 hours of quality time together.

Once again, as friendship is an art rather than a formula, you cannot simply start the clock, spend 300 hours with someone over a course of nine weeks and have an 'oven-ready' best friend at the end of it, but the research gives some fascinating insight into the amount of time friendship costs us to move through the circles of intimacy.

Time is critical for the best of friendships for several reasons, but probably most significantly for the necessity of conversation. Jesus is explicit about this link between friendship and communication in his extraordinary revelation to the disciples in John 15:15: 'I have called you friends, for everything that I learned from my Father I have made known to you.' The fact that he calls them friends is remarkable. That he has made known to them *everything* he has learned from the Father is astonishing. And the only way this was made possible was through hours of teaching, dialogue and discussion, on the road, over meals and in boats.

Without significant investment of time, our conversation does not have the opportunity to go beyond small talk and chit-chat to the 'deep and meaningfuls'. As author and leader Ajith Fernando states, 'By our inability to give time to listen we make it impossible for close friendship to develop . . . One of the keys to a deep friendship is time spent in long conversations.'[8] How we communicate well will be a consistent theme throughout the book, but at this point we need to be precise about the importance of time spent talking and listening to one another.

Time is precious. Spend it well.

2 Presence

Lament

When rumours of a virus turn to evening government updates.
When headlines move to daily news of fresh infection growth
    rates.
When schools are closed, then holidays postponed. Everyone's
    asking, 'Who has been furloughed?'
A slight change of plans, just wash your hands, 'It's like the flu,
    remember?'
Let's stay at home, do PE with Joe, it'll be over by September.
How long, O Lord?

When streets resemble ghost towns at peak lockdown regulation.
When we crave a crowd, cry out for connection from full-blown
    isolation.
When millions search for online church with new-found
    innovation.
Everything is online but getting loo roll is a hassle. And trust
    in power's eroded by trips to Barnard Castle.

It all ends in tiers, there's no quick fix. When you're a table
    of seven but there's a rule of six.
How long, O Lord?

When our dreams are dashed, ambitions strangled, our Christmas
    plans destroyed.
And a righteous anger rises at the murder of George Floyd.
When families are asked to grieve behind masks at graves
    of precious loved ones passed.
Life is in limbo, we are stuck in between, it's herd immunity
    or miracle vaccine.
2020 short-changed by Covid 19, and children aren't getting the
    food that they need.
How long, O Lord?

With ever-growing numbers of the daily deaths presented,
When this is the new normal, when what life was like lamented.
And will people stop using the word unprecedented?!
We are Zoomed out, home-schooled out, restrictions extended.
And those we love die unattended.
How long, O Lord?

I have been deprived of peace,
I have forgotten what prosperity is.
So I say my splendour is gone and all that I had hoped from the
    Lord.
My soul is downcast within me.

Yet this I call to mind and therefore I have hope:
Because of the Lord's great love we are not consumed, for his
    compassions never fail.
They are new every morning. Great is your faithfulness.

I wrote 'Lament' from a place of personal pain, just over a year into the coronavirus pandemic. We made it into a film, which went viral with over a thousand churches downloading it for online services and tens of thousands of views across social media platforms. I was surprised at how readily it was shared, and I received messages of thanks from many who had been 'asked to grieve behind masks at graves of precious loved ones past'. I have done a lot of reflecting on those months of the first lockdown in 2020 that were enveloped in disappointment, anxiety and bereavement. One of the conclusions I have reached is that they were so difficult because we were forced to journey through traumatic uncharted territory without the physical company of some of our closest friends and family.

We were not created to be socially distanced and when a deadly virus necessitated keeping one another at arm's length we lost our greatest comfort at the worst possible time. Presence.

> Piglet sidled up to Pooh from behind.
> 'Pooh!' he whispered.
> 'Yes, Piglet?'
> 'Nothing,' said Piglet, taking Pooh's paw. 'I just wanted to be sure of you.'[9]

I am so grateful that the most stringent social-distancing regulations for generations were introduced at a time when technology did all it could to make you feel as though you were speaking with someone face to face. It would have been a very different pandemic in the age of the fax machine, mobile phones the size of bricks, and pagers. But video conferencing, holographic projection, FaceTiming, Zooming, Skyping and virtual reality are no replacement for the real thing. Being in the same physical space as someone really matters. There is no shortcut to or substitute for proximity.

We all stand somewhere on the scale of 'I'll squeeze anything that moves' to 'Don't touch me'. Some of us wear 'Free Hugs' T-shirts, while others stand with crossed arms and legs. I have friends who embrace me and I am fortunate to escape with all my ribs intact. I have others who I know stepping within a metre of their personal space brings on a nervous sweat. Wherever we stand, the importance of touch in forming close human relationships cannot be overstated. Research into the early lives of babies has found that infants go into 'severe developmental decline' if they are not held, cradled and touched, receiving 'maternal care, maternal stimulation and maternal love'.[10] Touching moments appear throughout the gospels, as Jesus' hands met the afflicted skin of those labelled as untouchable and others reached out to touch the hem of his garment, believing that a moment of contact could change everything.

Presence matters because we are created with physical bodies with which we can look friends in the eyes and immediately sense something is wrong. We know the power of a reassuring arm round the shoulder or gentle hand on the back. I am the father of two sons who express their affection towards me by bundling me over and burying me in a pile of arms and legs on the living room floor. Their love language is fighting, but the bonding moments of playful wrestling are priceless.

For some, presence doesn't even have to be about touch. I have friends whose resistance to physical contact rivals others' enthusiasm for it. Some nationalities too are more touchy-feely than others. Britain is somewhat unsurprisingly behind Italy and France when it comes to appreciation of touch in a social setting, with Finland having the most enthusiastic huggers.[11] My dad died suddenly when I was 21. I cannot remember much of what anyone said to me during those tear-drenched hours that followed, but I remember vividly my friend Adam just *being* with me. That night I sat in my kitchen, unable to sleep. I was numb and unable to process the agony of the events of the previous twenty-four hours. My friend simply sat with me. Words were few, tears were abundant, and I will never forget the greatest gift he could have given me at that time: his presence.

This occasion illustrates the power of proximity at key moments in life and therein lies an important lesson in friendship. We will remember those who were with us, who chose to be near us, during life's key moments. Frodo Baggins tells the epitome of faithfulness and the companion who stubbornly refuses to leave his side, Samwise Gamgee, 'I am glad you are here with me. Here at the end of all things, Sam.'[12] Conversely we may also remember who was not there with us and for us. We may have other pressing concerns when a friend is in crisis. There may already be an arrangement in the diary when a friend's wedding invitation arrives on our doormat. But we must tread carefully. Great wisdom is required when balancing priorities between our own needs and the needs of those in our inner circles, especially during the accentuated, landmark life junctures.

Being present is an intentional gift that you give. It is a posture you adopt. Its enemy is distraction, which produces an absent-mindedness that leads to someone being physically in the room but mentally somewhere else. Occasionally my body has been sitting at dinner with my family, but my head and heart have been still at my desk working, still wandering through cyberspace or more likely still in a football stadium watching the game. Being tangibly present but emotionally absent can be more damaging to a relationship than not turning up at all. We communicate that our work or the sporting event taking place in our head is more important than the person right in front of us.

And if you really want to let the people around you know that you are dividing your presence between them and others, get your phone out. Research has shown that the mere presence of a phone on the table when two friends are connecting, even if the phone doesn't go off, has a detrimental effect on the interaction.[13] Can you imagine if Frodo had told Sam of his gratitude for his presence only to be greeted with a vacant grunt of acknowledgment as Sam posted a selfie on the Hobbiton group chat? Can you imagine how Adam's comfort to me would have been affected by his scrolling down a social media feed? Fighting these distractions is a battle worth fighting.

Being completely present is a choice worth making.

Sometimes the best thing you can do is not rush on to the next thing. 'Time is precious, but that is not why we don't linger. Our problem is that we are too restless.'[14] Some friendships develop because companions find an activity they love to do together. What often happens is that the activity becomes a sideshow for the friendship; it is the time spent in each other's company that matters. The best of friends eventually find that they can just be in each other's presence, sometimes not even talking or doing anything. To be with each other is enough.

No wonder the Bible tells us that Job's companions sat with him for a week in silence (Job 2:13). No wonder it was 'better' for Mary to sit at Jesus' feet than be busy making preparations (Luke 10:42). The wonder-full gift of Christmas is that God's salvation begins with the offering of himself. He is Immanuel, God with us (Matthew 1:23). The present is his presence. As we have received this gift of God's presence, as image-bearers we should pass it on. Let your with-ness be your witness. Presence matters.

3 Vulnerability

For the best of friends, time and presence are not enough. There are countless friendships and even marriages between people who spend a lot of time together but never achieve the kind of intimate connection needed to fulfil our deepest human longings and the closeness of relationship we were created for. Conversation rarely goes deeper than discussing the events of the day or the trivialities of other people's lives. Plans for the future are explored in terms of events and places rather than hopes and dreams. When deep and meaningful talk appears on the horizon, one or both parties make a U-turn and return the discourse to the superficial, frantically swimming for the surface like a panicked diver.

We were made for more.

There are greater depths of friendship we can all experience.

There are junction moments in relationships. As we have identified, they often begin with a connection, when you realize you have something in common. But as Jonathan Holmes identifies, 'few of us regularly enjoy a kind of friendship that extends much beyond a narrow range of shared activities and interests'.[15] Relationships that go deeper do not happen by accident. It is a much easier choice to keep our connections at a distance. When we imagine the circles of friends in the model we are exploring, the outer layers are filled with less pain, effort and cost. To move a friend closer to the centre of our universe takes time and presence. But the greatest cost is the jeopardy of making ourselves known.

'If you want acquaintances,' says author Rob Parsons, 'tell them your successes; if you want friends, tell them your fears.'[16] He identifies the key step on the journey towards having a friend at the centre of our circle: vulnerability. When we open our heart to another it is fuel on the friendship fire. But I am acutely aware that these words are far more easily written and read than they are put into practice. What is it about vulnerability that is so easy to celebrate but so difficult to apply?

We are afraid. I am afraid.

I want people to think I am strong, successful and sorted. I want to be a radiator rather than a drain. I want my Christian friends to think I am godly and wise. I want my not-yet-Christian friends to think I am cool and fun – the right kind of Christian. I wanted my parents to think I was the perfect son. I want my children to think I am the perfect dad.

I am not always these things. None of us are. Honesty is admitting this to ourselves. Vulnerability is admitting it to others.

We all have failures in our past, frustrations in our present and fears for the future. We can be scared that when we share these with others they will reject us, like us less and not want to spend time with us.

In the quiz show *Who Wants to Be a Millionaire?* contestants answer questions, and every correct answer increases the amount of money won until they reach £1 million. However, one incorrect answer and they lose it all, although there are a few 'safety nets' at various levels, guaranteeing they will leave with something if they pass certain points. The final safety net is £32,000, after which the money increases in eye-watering increments to £64,000, £125,000, £250,000 and £500,000. When you take the final jump, if you choose to answer the last question, the difference between a correct answer and an incorrect one is £968,000. There's a lot at stake.

Many of us have good friendships, but good is the enemy of great.[17] When we have a good relationship with someone, based on chemistry and common interests, these are like £125,000 friendships. We suspect, maybe even know, there could be more to a friendship, but we are afraid of losing what we have and worry that we might leave with a lot less. Fear prevents us from being vulnerable, taking conversation deeper, letting people in to know more about us. Overcoming our insecurities, reminding ourselves of our identity as a child of God with nothing to prove and opening up to someone can be an incredibly difficult and courageous thing to do.

And yet making ourselves known and revealing our heart to another can have a life-changing effect on us, our relationships and the other person. First, for us, the impact can bring a surprising freedom and joy where we were previously expecting shame and anxiety. When I have shared with others the ongoing pain of bereavement, frustrations at work, moral failures, sadness and disappointments, the effect has been healing and releasing. Second, the impact on the other can result in another, more profound, moment where the other cries, 'What? You too? I thought I was the only one.' Vulnerability begets vulnerability. The challenge is that so often neither party is ready to take the first step. And third, when we are in a community where this kind of openness becomes more and more normal, networks and friendship groups grow together as cords of intimacy and closeness tighten.

Of course, there are appropriate moments to be vulnerable and appropriate people to open up to. You may find that revealing your deepest and darkest secrets in a packed and quiet train carriage makes things a little awkward. The connection with time here is important. The kind of conversations where acquaintances become friends tend to take place on lengthy journeys or long into the night.

Discernment is also needed with who to open up to. When we make ourselves known we are building higher levels of trust. Vulnerability is giving the other person the power to destroy us and trusting them not to use it. It is sensible therefore to make it a gradual process, sense how we are received and if the other reciprocates.

There may be times when the vulnerability is not reciprocated – perhaps because the other is afraid or is not ready yet to build a higher level of trust. Perhaps the other has never engaged in that depth of conversation before. As Ajith Fernando notes, 'we get so used to small talk that it can be hard to stop and give time for serious and honest talk'.[18] I have several friends, some of whom I have known for many years, who remain £125,000 mates. With some there have been moments where I have shared my heart and tested deeper waters or asked questions that invite them to open up, but that door has remain closed. With these connections we must accept that they will stay in the outer circles of friendship for now. There may be a point in the future where a closer relationship develops, but our time would be better spent invested in others whom we might really get to know and make ourselves known to.

Jesus does not hide his heart from John. John sees the passionate anger of Jesus driving the money-changers out of the temple (John 2:13–17). He observes a vulnerable Jesus, as many disciples leave him, asking the Twelve, 'You do not want to leave too, do you?' (John 6:67). And then at the grave of Lazarus, three times John emphasizes the grief and compassion so evidently displayed by a man mourning for his friend (John 11:33, 35, 38). Jesus' relationship with the one he loved was one where he shared not just what he knew, but who he was. His example should encourage us to do the same with those closest to us.

Good to greater love

So in the dance of friendship there we have three of the most important steps: time, presence and vulnerability. As we begin to connect with others these are priceless movements, but they are also our currency as we invest in existing friendships and enjoy the company of the one or two in our closest circle. Before we move on from exploring the relationship at the centre of Jesus' earthly ministry, there is one final lesson John has to teach us.

His story is full of some of the most famous words in all of literature. 'For God so loved the world . . .' may well be the most read and spoken sentence of all time. The prologue that commences 'In the beginning was the Word . . .' has illuminated an immeasurable number of candlelit carol services. 'I am the way, the truth and the life' has been immortalized in song, evangelistic tract and billboard. But when it comes to human relationship, these are the most memorable words from the apostle's pen: 'Greater love has no one than this: to lay down one's life for one's friends' (John 15:13).

John knew what the most intimate of relationships looked like because he saw these words become action. Days after uttering them, Jesus would be crucified on a Roman cross to die in the place of the disciple he loved. John, like us, was a broken, sinful human being and Jesus bore the weight of John's pain, shame and guilt, and suffered physical agony and spiritual separation from the

Father for him. He then rose again to break the power of death over him and pave the way for his journey to heaven. John knew this was the best news in the world. He also witnessed the power of sacrifice.

For this story and this saviour, John then returned the favour. He responded to the invitation of his friend and laid his life down for him. We don't know the rest of his life's journey in great detail, but church historians tell us that John went on to lead and pastor the church Paul had founded in Ephesus, a city in ancient Greece and recipient of the book of Ephesians in the New Testament. When the church was persecuted by the Roman Empire under the emperor Domitian, John was exiled and imprisoned on the island of Patmos. His choice to follow Jesus, as for all of us, came with great adventure but also great cost.

This too is a hallmark of the best of friendships. Deep, unbreakable bonds between friends are forged by acts of sacrifice for one another when we choose to be generous and sacrificial with our time and finance, when we prefer the other and put the other's needs before our own. When we observe them repaying the favour and receive their generosity, these moments when we are surprised and humbled that someone would do this for us create in us deep connections that are difficult to forget and create reservoirs of trust.

The personal cost is worth it for this kind of friendship. In his reflection on the example of friendship between David and Jonathan, author Leonard Sweet observes, 'Most of all, a Jonathan sacrifices himself for you, even knowing, as the original Jonathan knew, that the more your song rises, the more his or her own song fades into the background.'[19] John watched on as John the Baptist embodied this, stepping back to propel Jesus' ministry forward, declaring, 'He must become greater; I must become less' (John 3:30). The strongest of relationships are formed where this is reflected in the hearts of two friends; they desire the best for one another and are prepared to lay their lives down to see that happen.

The best of amends: top friendship tips

Breaking the ice

What do you say when you meet someone for the first time?

There is an art to getting to know someone. Part of that art is asking the right questions, listening well to the answers and searching them for common ground on which to build. This is my favourite question when I meet someone for the first time: 'So what keeps you busy when you are not in <insert current location> on a <insert current day of the week>?'

I have found this the single best question to break the ice and find out about someone's life and passions. Whether they are most enthusiastic about their job, hobbies or pets, this question helps unearth it. If people are retired or unemployed, they don't feel awkward that they don't have a profession to talk about. Their answer will provide you with either a shared passion or interest to build from, or something you know nothing about and can be genuinely interested in.

If the former is the case, let the person know that you share that enthusiasm, but resist the temptation to reel off your credentials or knowledge at this stage. Instead ask more questions and keep listening well. There are few things that make someone feel accepted and loved as much as being listened to.

If someone reveals a job or hobby that you know nothing or little about, then a great follow-up question begins, 'Tell me more about . . .' Open-ended invitations like this mean you rarely get a monosyllabic answer and you give permission for the other to begin to open the door to his or her life to you.

Be present

Priya Parker is a gathering expert. She says: 'Anyone who gathers nowadays must, like it or not, cope with the reality that people are often elsewhere, thanks to their technological devices. Perpetual distraction is a curse of modern life and of modern convening in particular.'[20]

In this chapter we have considered the gift of being present to those around us. What might this look like in practice?

- Consider making the family meal table a phone-free zone. No phones are allowed at the Knox family dinner table. Not even my younger son's fake plastic Paw Patrol one that makes dog noises when you press the keys. Especially not my younger son's fake plastic Paw Patrol one that makes dog noises when you press the keys.
- Go off-grid when you go on holiday. When we go away as a family, I choose to disconnect from not just my work world but the social media arena and the news and sport headlines. In those precious moments of walking and playing games with my family, I don't want to be distracted by a football score or a picture of what my friend from school is having for dinner.
- When you meet someone for coffee put your phone in your pocket. Tell the person you are doing so. I have to fight hard enough not to look over someone's shoulder to people-watch as I listen to what is being said. I want to communicate that he or she has my undivided attention. This state of play is shattered by a mere glance at the flickering screen on the table. The text, email, call or notification can wait.
- Embrace curfews, Sabbaths and sabbaticals from your phone and/or its features. A screen curfew at least an hour before bed will help you sleep better, as well as help you be present to those around you.[21] Have a day a week without your phone. Make arrangements in advance and be unapologetically with those you spend the day with. Take a week or two off socials. I often remove social media platforms from my home screen between Christmas and New Year to be present with family and friends.

The cost of not knowing what my work colleagues got for Christmas is worth every thumb swipe. If I'm friends with them I can ask them in the New Year. If not, then that's always a good question to ask.

The themes of this chapter can be explored further using small-group resources, videos and discussion questions. Delve deeper at: www.philknox.co.uk

Further reading

A. Fernando, *Reclaiming Friendship* (IVP, Leicester, 1991). This is a hidden gem that challenges and stretches you as a friend.

J. Holmes, *The Company We Keep: In Search of Biblical Friendship* (Cruciform Press, Minneapolis, MN, 2014). A similar work to Vaughan Roberts's book on Christian friendship, but more expansive. Biblical and helpful.

L. Sweet, *11* (David C. Cook, Colorado Springs CO, 2008). A stunning book that encourages you to take inspiration from biblical figures for the types of relationship you need in your life. When this was published I bought eleven copies to give to my closest companions.

5

Three – Jesus had an inner circle

Though one may be overpowered, two can defend themselves.
A cord of three strands is not quickly broken.
(Ecclesiastes 4:12)

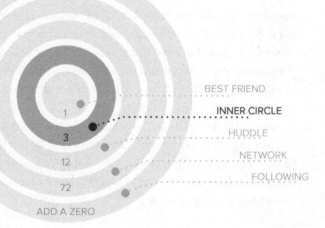

Jos, our younger son, is working out where his boundaries lie. He is
very protective over his car collection, and stewards his affection with
the same level of diligence and passion. At the moment, when I tell
him I love him, his response is defiant: 'No you don't! Mummy loves
me!' When his older brother expresses the same display of emotion,
Jos similarly tells him that his mother has the monopoly on the rights
to be able to love him. Soon (we hope) there will come a day when Jos
realizes that he is able to be loved by more than one person.

This is the beauty of friendship. It is not like marriage. There is no 'forsaking all others', as the wedding vows dictate.

Two's company; three, four and five are allowed.

Strength in numbers

I recently spent the weekend away with four old friends. We live in different areas of the country and met in a remote cottage to catch up, watch football, eat steak and drink whiskey. We didn't all arrive at once. In true reunion style, we drove there in separate cars and met each other in ones and twos. I was fascinated by the changing dynamic as our party grew in number. As each person arrived to a rapturous (and boisterous) welcome, the electric energy increased in the group to be ever greater than the sum of its parts. A third person in a marriage spells disaster. In circles of friends, there are advantages to addition. As C. S. Lewis notes, 'Friendship is the least jealous of loves. Two friends delight to be joined by a third, and three by a fourth, if only the newcomer is qualified to become a real friend.'[1]

It is worth emphasizing that Jesus did not simply seek out a teammate. His approach to changing the world was more *Avengers Assemble* than *Batman & Robin*. Just as our friendships are poorer if we lack quality connections in the innermost circles, we can be equally imbalanced if we focus all of our energies on one or two people. Beyond the disciple he loved, Jesus models for us a variety of depths of connection. In this chapter we are exploring the next layer of his relationships – the few friends he kept closest to his side, namely Peter, James and John.

Inclusivity versus exclusivity

Friendship is both inclusive and exclusive. Having just made the case for the more the merrier when it comes to friendship circles, I am now going to suggest that this is held in tension by the fact that choosing friends also creates necessary boundaries. This is a key paradox that we must wrestle and be reconciled with. Jesus was the epitome of inclusivity. 'Come to me, *all* you who are weary and burdened' (Matthew 11:28, emphasis added). He welcomed women and children in an age when they were lucky to be seen, let alone heard. And yet the way he conducted his relationships was to pick some above others. Peter, James and John were members of an extremely exclusive club.

There are several places in the gospels where we read of times when Jesus is just with these three fishermen. The rest of the disciples are nowhere to be seen. Significantly, as we will see, these are often important and intimate moments that become key episodes in the life story. The precedent is set in Mark 5. Jesus is surrounded by crowds in the midst of a teaching and healing tour around Galilee. On the way to the house of a synagogue leader called Jairus, he heals a sick woman who has been bleeding for twelve years. She receives restoration by reaching out to touch his cloak. As he approaches Jairus's house, Mark states, '*he did not let anyone follow him* except Peter, James and John the brother of James' (Mark 5:37, emphasis added).

Let's stop for a moment and consider how this would have felt if you were Thomas. Andrew, Peter's brother, would probably have asked, 'Why does one sibling get to go and not the other?' There was another James in the Twelve, whom we know as 'Son of Alpheus'. He may have stepped forward on hearing his name, only to realize to his disappointment it was the other one. Perhaps this was the moment resentment began to form in Judas Iscariot's heart. 'He did not let anyone follow him except . . .' is really exclusive language. It is only Peter, James, John and Jesus who proceed into the home of the synagogue leader, where they witness the resurrection of his daughter.

The next rendezvous of the 'fab four' in Mark's account occurs when Jesus takes them on an off-site trip up a mountain. In an episode known as the transfiguration, the inner circle trek up a high peak (thought to be either Mount Tabor or Mount Hermon), where Jesus is displayed in his glory and hears the affirmation of his Father.

This is an important encounter for the Son of God. To receive the validating words of the Father over his earthly life and ministry is a deep and intimate moment. To be reminded of the significance of his place in the story as Moses and Elijah appear, representing the law and the prophets he has come to fulfil, makes this a profound and pronounced event. Peter, James and John would have been under no illusion as to just how special it was for them to witness it. No wonder Peter says to Jesus, 'It is good for us to be here' (Mark 9:5).

Imagine the moment the privileged three return to the nine left behind and report on what happened. It is not a surprise that shortly after this event Jesus asks them what they were arguing about on the road to Capernaum (Mark 9:33). His question is met with an awkward, sheepish silence, as they have been arguing about who is the greatest. You can picture Peter making his case: 'Did you see how the Rabbi chose me to climb the mountain to meet Elijah? He'll probably ask me to die with him.'

The three fishermen appear next together in Mark 13 in a private conversation with Jesus, this time joined by Peter's brother Andrew (clearly by this time he has made his case to Jesus that if John gets a 'plus one' at the top table so should his sibling).

Jesus reconvenes the inner circle one last time in the intense and dramatic build-up to his betrayal, trial and execution. The backdrop is Gethsemane, the scene of the lowest ebb of Jesus' emotions. In his deep distress, bearing a troubled heart and an overwhelmed soul, what does he do? He seems to deliberately leave most of the disciples behind and calls upon Peter, James and John to go with him, further into the garden, to be with him in his hour of greatest emotional need.

Drawing the lines somewhere

We have to grasp the uncomfortable nettle that Jesus did not treat all of his friends in the same way. This is the tension that we must not only grapple with, but also apply to our relational circles:

1 The kingdom of God is scandalously, beautifully and counter-culturally inclusive We are called to have open hearts and generous spirits in how we relate to others, treating everyone we come across with a God-given grace and winsome welcome. There are also no boundaries to whom we should befriend, regardless of their history, nationality, ethnicity, sexuality, political extremity or religiosity, following the example of the Nazarene known as a 'friend of . . . sinners' (Luke 7:34). His example is that of radical, audacious friendship with the most privileged to the most broken, knowing that acceptance does not necessarily equate to approval.

2 We are finite human beings in a restricted space with a limited amount of time and emotional energy This means there are points on our journey where we must 'not let anyone follow us' except a select few. It means our mountains will be too crowded if everyone is there. It means that in our Gethsemanes we must leave some at a certain point and only go deeper with an inner circle.

My parents would unapologetically tell us that we were stuck with them, echoing Harper Lee's sentiment that 'you sho' can't choose your family', but your friends are up to you.[2] C. S. Lewis discerns that some have a hostility to friendship, 'because it is selective and the affair of the few. To say, "These are my friends" implies, "Those are not."'[3] This can be what makes friendship so painful yet also so prized: 'Friendship is uniquely precious: our friends are the ones we've chosen, the elected few.'[4]

This relational radius

How big is this circle? For Jesus it was three. D'Artagnan has the Three Musketeers. Harry has Ron and Hermione. The Boy has the Mole, the Fox and the Horse. Robin Dunbar extends this number up to five. Ross, Rachel, Phoebe, Chandler, Monica and Joey each has five. In the wakc of the coronavirus pandemic, when the UK emerged from its first lockdown and social distancing rules were relaxed, the government introduced a 'rule of six' to allow people to meet in groups but limit the rapid spread of the virus. Although primarily driven by epidemiology, the number seems far from accidental in terms of six being an important number for social dynamic. Priya Parker agrees: 'Groups of this rough size are wonderfully conducive to intimacy, high levels of sharing, and discussion through storytelling.'[5]

A sensible range seems to be three to five. In this circle, contact is often at least weekly and the investment in terms of time, presence and vulnerability is high. These friends may or may not know each other. Interestingly, in the examples we have shared, they do, with friendship connections between the others in the group forming a mini network in a tightly knit band. This will be the case for some, but for others, their inner circle will be aware of each other but may not share such mutual intimacy. Often if someone has moved around a lot geographically, significant connections may have been made in various places, which are maintained through regular contact, and these individual friendships form the person's closest sphere. Others form a dynamic group with people they grow up with or meet at university, work, sports club or church, and this lays the foundation for their inner circle. My uncle's band of brothers is made up of a group of four men who formed a ten-pin bowling team in the 1970s. They have journeyed through the joys and heartaches of life together for over fifty years.

What does friendship look like with those who are this close to us? What can we learn from Jesus, Peter, James and John?

The valley and the mountaintop

A significant proportion of my life in ministry has been spent leading teams and speaking at festivals, camps and weekends away. I spent so long at one particular outdoor activity centre that they threatened to name an accommodation lodge after me (I'm still waiting for my invite to cut the ribbon to open the 'Knox Suite'). In these fields, marquees, log cabins and mud pits I have seen God do extraordinary things. There have been 'heaven meets earth' times of worship, miraculous breakthroughs and irrefutable answers to prayer, and my favourite thing of all – watching countless people choose to become followers of Jesus. At the end of these weeks I often give a little speech to the team I have been part of for the precious preceding days, encouraging them to *treasure* the encounters they have experienced.

These have been mountaintop moments, I would emphasize, but life is not lived on the metaphorical mountain. Life is mostly lived on the plain, in an often mundane rhythm of necessary normality. Then, sadly all too often, we find ourselves in the depths of the valley: drowning in discouragement, bereavement, disappointment and pain. From the despair of the valley and the humdrum, relentless grind of the plain it can be difficult to remember the mountaintop, let alone see it. This has been a helpful metaphor for me as I have contemplated the seasons of life I find myself in.

Back to Peter, James and John. It is of great significance that the times Jesus deliberately invites his inner circle to be with him are the mountaintop and valley moments of his earthly ministry, both symbolically and literally. The transfiguration takes place on a peak, Gethsemane is at the foot of the Mount of Olives. They are literally the highs and lows of his life. Interestingly, 'Gethsemane' literally means 'oil press'. It is the place where Jesus is placed under the most intense stresses and burdens.

Celebrate the highs of your life with your inner circle. For most of us, there are precious few mountaintop moments to enjoy, so when they come along share them first with a call to the people who mean the most to you rather than in a post on your social media. New jobs, new babies, new Christians, birthdays, engagements, beginnings, ends and milestones call for feasting and festivities. Throw the invitations as wide as your circles, sensibilities and budget allow, but put your closest friends at the top of the list and organize the date around them.

The fight of your life

Do not isolate yourself when your soul is overwhelmed. In the agony of grief and the disorientation of a crisis I have felt a strong temptation to withdraw from all forms of contact. At times this has been a physical response to shut the door to my room, sit in the middle of the bed and pull the duvet over my head. It is natural to want to disconnect, detach and disengage as we cling to self-preservation.

At the same time, you may be faced with an overwhelming number of generous offers from friends reaching out to help: 'If there's anything I can do . . .' In the fight of life, as I have been reeling from its occasionally brutal blows and have found myself on the ropes, there are two or three people's voices I want to hear speaking to me in my corner of the ring. Their voices, encouragement, grace and presence have made all the difference, helped me to my feet again, and caused me to not throw in the towel.

A friend loves at all times,
and a brother is born for a time of adversity.
(Proverbs 17:17)

Life is a battle. We need comrades for the conflict. At war with the Amalekites, the Israelite warriors were winning when Moses stood over the struggle with his arms upraised (Exodus 17:8–16). To prevent his arms from falling when they grew tired, Aaron and Hur, Moses' inner circle, held his hands in the air. In the film *Gladiator*, the hero Maximus is thrown into the arena with several fellow slaves to be butchered by trained soldiers in a re-enactment of an ancient battle. The slaves convene and wait, weaponless sitting ducks, surrounded by a baying crowd and gates about to unleash their fate. Maximus rallies his cohort, telling them that whatever comes out of the gates they've got a better chance of survival if they work together. When we are besieged by bereavement and hard pressed on every side, it is our closest friends who hold up our arms and surround us with shields. We do not and should not invite every friend on our social media platform into the arena, but we must ask our most trusted companions to walk through the valley with us. 'Though one may be overpowered, two can defend themselves' (Ecclesiastes 4:12).

When we fall

Life's pains do not always come from circumstances conspiring against us or by the hand of another. They are often self-inflicted. When we let ourselves down, make a reckless choice or lose the internal battle between temptation and will power, this can feel like a very different valley from the one where it's not our fault. And yet we need those same friends with us anyway.

At several points in my life I have made a terrible decision. I have been embarrassingly selfish. Often, when I think I have control and discipline over one potential area of weakness in my life, the enemy finds another vulnerability to try to exploit. Sin is so powerful, so destructive and always lurking in the next room, ready to wreak its havoc if we open the door.

The great news is that if we know Jesus, we are no longer slaves to it (Romans 6:6), and my experience is that, as I have matured, not only have I sinned less, but I am quicker to recover from times when I have got things wrong. A common biblical image for sinning is falling or stumbling on the road. In these terms, not only have I stayed on my feet longer, but I have got better at getting back to my feet and dusting myself down after tripping up. Proverbs 24:16 reminds us that 'though the righteous fall seven times, they rise again'. And in this process, the help of friends is just as important as when we are besieged by external hardships.

The biggest battle can be talking to those in our inner circle about what we have done. I remember just how nervous I was one cold morning when over a cup of tea I spoke to Adam about a mess I had got myself into. 'Mate, I need to tell you something . . .' The internal fight within me raged. I prefer it when he thinks I'm the epitome of holiness. I'm tempted to deal in half-truths, to sugar coat my failings and deflect blame away from myself. But the relief of laying it out before a friend I trust was an important step and it helped me back to my feet.

When we confess our sins to one another we break a significant amount of their power over our lives (James 5:16). We also help protect ourselves from making matters worse. Isolation can increase and intensify a downward spiral. Have you noticed that when the snake approaches Eve in the garden of Eden she is alone? The enemy knows that we are far more vulnerable when we are isolated. In Gethsemane, Jesus is not only tormented, but he is also tempted to back away from his destiny: 'Take this cup from me' (Mark 14:36). Perhaps the company of Peter, James and John is not just to provide comfort for him, but to remind him of the people he is about to go to the torturous cross for.

Our inner circle gives us perspective. When we blow it in one area of our lives, it can be easy to catastrophize and feel that we are a failure in every area of our lives. Friends who know us well can help us to take a step back and see the bigger picture, speaking truth of who we are and whose we are, and reminding us of our strengths and successes.

They also give us accountability. Our failure could be part of, or the beginning of, a pattern of repeated destructive behaviour. Journeying with someone honestly gives us a much better chance of denying sin a stranglehold in our lives. Knowing that the next time we see this friend we are going to have to look them in the eye and give account for our actions in this area can be a powerful deterrent and help us keep our behaviour and lifestyle healthy.

In life it is not a matter of if we fall, but when. How often and how heavily is down to us, but we are kidding ourselves, and those closest to us, if we think we can stay on our feet for ever. Ecclesiastes encourages us that two are better than one: 'if either of them falls down, one can help the other up' (Ecclesiastes 4:10). It is not always appropriate to publish our self-inflicted pain to every layer of the friendship circle, but being real about our failures with our close friends is invaluable.

When we hurt each other

If you think you are having a bad day, consider those behind these expensive mistakes.

- In 2014, the French rail company SNCF made 2,000 new trains without measuring their width correctly. As a result they were too wide for many of Europe's tunnels, stations and platforms. It cost over €14 billion to fix the problem.
- In 1980, an engineer in Louisiana got his coordinates mixed up, sending Texaco engineers to the wrong location. Instead of hitting oil, the drill hit a salt mine, causing the obliteration of the tunnels and the depth of the lake to increase from 6 feet to 200 feet in a matter of hours. The oil company was forced to pay $45 million to make amends.
- In 2013, IT worker James Howells threw out his computer hard drive at a waste disposal site in Newport, Wales. It contained cryptocurrency that at the time was not worth very much but has since increased dramatically in value to being worth over £340 million at the time of writing. Despite petitioning his local council and lining up engineers to recover the data, he is not allowed to search the landfill site to look for his Bitcoin treasure trove.

Yet when our relationships end, the loss can feel even more costly. The pain can even be physical. Social psychologist Naomi Eisenberger conducted an experiment involving a virtual game of catch that simulated social rejection by the subject being excluded from being thrown the virtual ball. She measured the effect by scanning the brains of those in the experiment and found that the areas of our brains activated when we experience social exclusion are the same as those where we perceive physical pain.[6] When we are rejected by our friends, when our relationships break down, our hearts may only break metaphorically, but the emotional agony we feel is real. It can be measured.

Friendships usually end in one of two distinctly different styles: either a long-drawn-out fizzle or an explosive bang. As you reflect on your circles of friends, there may be some whose direction of travel you have observed moving steadily towards your inner circles, but there may be others who have been closer to you but whose trajectory is now unmistakably gradually headed towards the outer rings. The gradual fading out of friendships seems to be more common than with romantic relationships, mostly because of the lack of exclusivity. If you want to be friends with someone else, you don't have to dump all your other friends first to avoid cheating on them.

But that doesn't diminish the amount of pain we can cause or damage we can do to those close relational connections. When we spend long periods of time in the presence of others, building reservoirs of trust and opening up caverns of vulnerability, we expose ourselves to being hurt and let down, and many of us will have experienced the heartache of being injured by a friend. If you want to know how it's done, here are three sure-fire ways of damaging a friendship. (To be a good friend, do the opposite.)

1 Gossip Information is power and if you want to win a quick hearing and flimsy favour with someone, gossiping about others will help to make you a cheap connection. Solomon tells us, 'The words of a gossip are like choice morsels' (Proverbs 18:8). But just as a healthy body cannot be built on snacks and fast food, scandal and slander will never build the trust required for a lasting friendship. In fact they will work against it. Proverbs tells us elsewhere, 'A perverse person stirs up conflict, and a gossip separates close friends' (Proverbs 16:28) and warns us, 'A gossip betrays a confidence; so avoid anyone who talks too much' (Proverbs 20:19). If you don't want a close friend to be vulnerable with you again, passing on trusted and privileged information to others is a proven way of stemming the flow.

2 Make a friendship feel as one-sided as possible Podcasters and authors Aminatou Sow and Ann Friedman frame the building of a relationship in terms of stretching.[7] As friendships develop over time, and as circumstances change, give and take is required as friends make sacrifices for one another. For example, if one makes a big geographical move, gets married, becomes a parent or develops a taste for a box-set you hate, the friendship will need to be flexible and supple enough to cope with that stretch.

As a friendship stretches, there needs to be a degree of equality of give and take between the friends. Sow and Friedman expand this: 'The amount of stretching doesn't have to feel equal in every single moment – sometimes one person will require more from the friendship than the other – but over time, the *give* has to even out with the *take*.'[8]

This is an important dynamic to bear in mind when investing in an embryonic friendship. It's also a reality for relationships that have lasted for decades. The muscles in these friendships may be able to stretch further, but they can still tear if taken for granted.

One thing is for sure: if you do want to harm a relationship, make sure the other person is doing all the stretching. Never reply to their text messages or return their calls. Always meet them on your terms. Make as little effort as possible. Always forget their birthday.

3 Break your promises In recent years we have seen an erosion of trust in many of the institutions we are asked to put our trust in. The biggest reason for this is a lack of integrity. Integrity is doing the right thing even if no-one is looking. It is living by the rules you expect others to abide by and doing what you say you will do. It is a critical ingredient in healthy relationships.

If you want to initiate the breakdown in a relationship, make some promises and then break them. Arrange to meet your friend somewhere and don't turn up. Lie about where you are and what you are doing.

Just to be clear, in case you are skim-reading and missed the preceding paragraph, these are things *not* to do!

When 'the rock' crumbles

Peter was in Jesus' inner circle. He was only called Peter because Jesus changed his name. Before that he was called Simon, which means 'pliable and reed-like', but in a destiny-changing speech at Caesarea Philippi, Jesus told Peter he would be the rock on which his church would be built (Matthew 16:18). Like all of us, the rock was a work in progress and if you were looking for more top tips on how to damage a friendship, Peter had a 'few he made earlier'. At the aforementioned high of Jesus' ministry, as Moses and Elijah appeared, Peter ruined the moment with a silly comment about making little houses for them (Mark 9:5). In the hour of Jesus' great need as he sweat blood in anguish, having specifically requested that Peter come with him his friend fell asleep. And then, taken directly from the 'broken promises' playbook, he said he would go with Jesus to his death, before denying him three times.

But this gives us an opportunity to gain insight from the best of friends as Jesus responded to the failure of his 'rock'.

True forgiveness

Forgiveness is a vital but often overlooked aspect of friendship. When it comes to hurting those closest to us, in our broken, fallen humanity it is often a case of not if but when. If we decide to cut and run the moment we get hurt, we may find our friendships resemble revolving doors rather than towers of strength. But what is forgiveness and what does it look like for friends?

First, it is absolutely necessary, primarily for the friend who has been hurt. Bitterness and resentment are potent, dangerous and joy-stealing, and they make us less loving and less loveable. Unforgiveness, so the saying goes, is like drinking poison and waiting for the other person to die. There's a reason we pray, 'Forgive us our sins as we forgive those . . .'

Second, it's a choice. Sometimes we need to forgive people who have not even said they are sorry. The most difficult person I chose to forgive died without ever being able to express remorse. Forgiveness is as much for our benefit as for the other person. We might not feel ready, but we can begin the journey by telling God how we feel, deciding and declaring, 'I choose to forgive this person. I will not give bitterness a home in my heart.'

Third, it is not the same as restoration and reconciliation. These may come but will happen afterwards and take longer. Peter's crime against Jesus is treacherous. After three years of intimate friendship, investment, meals, journeys, trust and vulnerability, he knowingly denies he even knows his rabbi and mentor. He is forgiven with the rest of us at the cross. When Jesus speaks the words 'Father, forgive them' from the place called The Skull, he does so prophetically over the cosmos, past, present and future. Peter is then restored and reconciled to the resurrected Jesus at a beach breakfast in John 21.

When they had finished eating, Jesus said to Simon Peter, 'Simon son of John, do you love me more than these?'

'Yes, Lord,' he said, 'you know that I love you.'

Jesus said, 'Feed my lambs.'

Again Jesus said, 'Simon son of John, do you love me?'

He answered, 'Yes, Lord, you know that I love you.'

Jesus said, 'Take care of my sheep.'
The third time he said to him, 'Simon son of John, do you love me?'
(vv. 15–17)

This interchange is a deliberate journey on Jesus' part. Peter gets the opportunity to reaffirm his love for Jesus three times, once for each of his denials. In instructing Peter to take care of the sheep, Jesus is reminding him of his destiny. His identity as 'the rock' is still intact. His connection to the original good shepherd is restored, and he will carry the crook-shaped baton on the next lap of the race.

All wrongs in friendships should lead to forgiveness. It is important to state that not all should lead to restoration and reconciliation. Where relationships have been toxic and abusive we must forgive, but it is not always wise to return to a close relationship that does not bring the best out in us.

Fourth, forgiveness between friends is a gift that must be graciously and gratefully received. I am frequently deeply moved when I imagine the series of events from Peter's perspective. He 'weeps bitterly' when he realizes what he has done (Luke 22:62), then has the agony of watching the friend he has just let down be brutally and gruesomely executed. To have your hopes and dreams dashed regarding what Jesus might mean for your future is one thing, but that must have been miserably compounded by bitter personal sorrow with the regret he felt. Imagine him heaving fish into the boat and then hope erupting in his heart as he realizes through tired eyes that his friend is alive. After a reunion to surely rival the return of the prodigal son in its emotional embrace, Peter must then respond to Jesus' repetitive questioning and reiterate his love. To both reconcile and be reconciled requires a dose of humility and honesty.

When we get things wrong in a friendship we must say sorry and ask for forgiveness. When someone apologizes to us we must accept the apology and express forgiveness. From that point restoration and reconciliation can be pursued. It may take time for confidence in one another to be re-established, especially if the wrongdoing was a particularly large breach of trust, but it is possible. Love really does cover over all wrongs (see Proverbs 10:12) and in the long term, friendships can be stronger for having passed through these storms. Peter follows Jesus to the end of his days, eventually fulfilling his promise to die for his name, probably crucified by Nero in Rome in AD 64.

The best of amends: top friendship tips

What to do when the proverbial hits the fan

We have spoken a great deal in this chapter about the importance of allowing friends to be with us in our time of need, but what does this look like practically?

Texting is okay, phone calls are good, video calls even better, but being with one another in person is best. When my mum died in 2020, I was inundated with messages of comfort, assurances of prayer and offers of, 'If there's anything I can do . . .' First, do not underestimate the power of this. If you are praying, if you can offer help, let the person know. It means a great deal.

Second, as the person needing the company I had to fight against my inclination to isolate myself. I accepted the offer of my closest friends to come and see me to talk, sit and grieve together. I organized to meet with a couple of friends and walk together. Do not underestimate the cost of this. Walking with someone closely through acute pain requires great faithfulness, time and emotional energy. This is why we can only do it meaningfully for those in our inner circle. Here is Ajith Fernando again:

Few people are willing to pay the price in terms of the time needed to help a friend with a personal problem. It takes time and patience to listen to friends sharing their problems, to comfort those who are sorrowful and to counsel those in need of guidance.[9]

Good news people

We've spent a lot of this chapter in the valley. Here is some advice for the mountaintop.

1 When you have good news to share, entrust it first to your inner circle 'Rejoice with me' (Luke 15:9). This makes them feel privileged and allows them to share in your joy. We are more likely to text good news and to call people to tell them the bad. However you communicate it, let your closest friends know first – from promotions to engagements to the smallest answer to prayer. We desperately need to be good news people in a bad news world.

2 When something good happens to one of your friends, celebrate well with them Life is full of too many disappointments and discouragements not to rejoice when good news is shared. Beware of comparison when this happens. Love is not jealous (1 Corinthians 13:4), but we can easily be envious of friends' successes. Pastor and author Robert Madu has coined the phrase 'Comparison will consistently cloud the clarity of your calling'.[10] It will also prevent you from being the best of friends. Be generous and exuberant in celebration with them. Tell them how proud you are of them. Better to be accused of being too extravagant in celebrating a friend than to be underwhelming.

Summary

Mountaintops.
   Valleys.
   We need the best of friends in both.

This is the inner circle. It is built for the highs and lows of life. Peter, James and John were close companions of Jesus, intimately involved in his day-to-day ministry, but they went further than everyone else and were invited to share in the best and worst of times. We can have expansive friendships, but we desperately need a few to stand with us on the mountaintops, comfort us in our Gethsemanes, lift our arms in our battles, share our failings and fallings with us, and forgive us as we forgive them.

Our horizons are about to expand. Let's invite the huddle to join us.

The themes of this chapter can be explored further using small-group resources, videos and discussion questions. Delve deeper at: www.philknox.co.uk

Further reading

W. Hill, *Spiritual Friendship: Finding love in the church as a celibate gay Christian* (Brazos Press, Grand Rapids MI, 2015). Wes challenges and inspires his readers to deeper community and to especially make room for those who are single, by choice or situation.

C. S. Lewis, *The Four Loves* (William Collins, London, 2012). Much quoted in this book, and worth buying just for the chapter on friendship, Lewis warmly and winsomely plumbs profound relational depths.

6

Twelve – Jesus had a huddle

Nobody talks about Jesus' miracle of having 12 close friends in his 30s.
(Unknown)

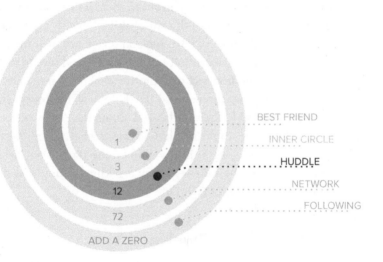

Beginnings are beautiful. I love the start of things. I am a morning person. I get excited about New Year. I live for the dawn, the opening of the curtains on the first day of holiday, the hush of a theatre as the lights dim, the referee's kick-off whistle and the roar of the crowd, the high-pitched revving of engines with 'It's lights out and away we go . . .'

When I meet good friends I love to ask them how they met, what drew them to each other and the formative shared events that have caused them to co-star on each other's storyboards. The beginnings of groups of friends are equally fascinating. Great works of literature and film are built on compelling relational origin stories. The Fellowship of the Ring, a band of brothers made up of hobbits, men, a dwarf, an elf and a wizard, is formed from a crisis meeting at the Council of Elrond in J. R. R. Tolkien's *The Lord of the Rings*, when deciding what to do with the ring of power. The Avengers are assembled by SHIELD when Loki invades the earth. The opening scenes of the *Oceans* movies are exquisitely constructed as the teams are recruited for the eight-, eleven-, twelve- and thirteen-person heists.

In the narrative arc of eternity, however, there is one team to rule them all. Its members were not the super-skilled, highly trained or genetically amended heroes of a Hollywood script, but their impact was greater than any collaboration in history. I would love to have been there as the band first met one another, when the inner circle were joined by Andrew, Thomas and Bartholomew; to observe the dynamic changing as Matthew, Judas and Simon the Zealot entered the room. These men would not have known what was about to happen to them. These beginnings would be the start of an extraordinary, world-defining journey. They are known simply as the Twelve, and they formed Jesus' huddle.

Twelve

Gathering expert Priya Parker explains that there are certain 'magic numbers' in groups. Something powerful happens in a group dynamic of twelve to fifteen people. There are twelve seats around King Arthur's famous table and in a jury box. Twelve to fifteen is the size of the smallest military unit and the size of many sports teams. Most political cabinets have this many seats around the decision-making table. 'Twelve is small enough to build trust and intimacy, and small enough for a single moderator, if there is one, formal or informal, to handle.'[1] And yet it is large enough, as we will discover, to include sufficient diversity to enrich the group. When Jesus chose twelve, he was pressing home his advantage of his intimate knowledge of how human dynamics work.

What is special about this layer of friendship? In some ways this is the middle ground of friendship. You are not as close to these individuals as you are to your inner circle, but you are significantly more intimate and vulnerable with them than you are with the next outward layer, where the numbers begin to increase dramatically. This circle may contain friends you have been best friends with in the past, there may be years of history between you, you are likely to be in regular, at least monthly, contact with them and when you spend time together it is easy, fun and life-giving. This layer may also contain clusters of friends with whom you share mutual connection, like Jesus' apostles. When I look at my huddle, I smile from name to name and it is easy to remember the joy of shared experiences. I know them well and they know me.

But what can we learn from how Jesus created his huddle and who was in it?

You can choose your friends

One of my favourite sketches as a teenager featured a character called 'Indecisive Dave'. The source of the comedy was two of Dave's friends presenting him with two opposing views and him flip-flopping between them with the utmost certainty, continually agreeing and disagreeing with himself. By the end of the sketch, Dave would be so exasperated and infuriated by his own indecision that he would exclaim, 'I don't know what I want!' I would be crying with laughter.

Choice is stressful. The ever-deafening narrative of individualism has led us to believe that more choice is always a good thing, that it enhances our freedom and autonomy, but it is also making us more anxious and escalating our expectations.[2] In 2015, a leading UK supermarket decided to take 30,000 products off its shelves as it felt that offering shoppers choice between 28 tomato ketchups and 224 kinds of air freshener was not helping their mental well-being.[3] We all vary in our decision-making process. Some of us are impulsive and make instant, gut decisions; others agonize for days and resemble Dave in their indecision. One of the challenges of friendship, as we are discovering, is that who we spend time with matters greatly, and we have to make good choices in who we invest our time in. The example of Jesus is to take time to make this decision well.

Jesus was prayerful, thoughtful and deliberative in selecting his huddle. Luke recalls that before calling this group together, the Son of God 'went out to a mountainside to pray, and spent the night praying to God' (Luke 6:12). The connection between this and what Luke tells us happened immediately afterwards is obvious. In the very next verse we hear that Jesus called his disciples to him and appointed the Twelve. Jesus is God. He is the wisest human being who ever lived. And yet he needs to spend a whole night alone in prayer before choosing those he will devote his time and energy to in the coming years.

Wisdom is needed in choosing those we will spend our time with. Proverbs 13:20 advises us, 'Walk with the wise and become wise, for a companion of fools suffers harm.' There is a curious tension in friendship where you have the opportunity to influence and open yourself up to be influenced by your friends. Perhaps this is most obvious in speech. My wife is a stranger far from home. She is an Essex girl in exile in Birmingham, a missionary to the Midlands. As such, in the last twenty years her accent has softened. Recently one of our best friends stopped by for a cup of tea. As Dani started talking he interrupted with, 'Dani, have you been talking to your family?'

'Yes,' she answered. 'How did you know?'

'You sound loads more Essex than usual.'

There is a magnetism about friendship. We are not only drawn, often powerfully, in other people's direction, but once in their presence, we can pick up some of their electric charge, as well as depositing some of our own on them. Our close companions influence the way we behave, think and speak. Those we spend time with will shape the person we become. Those we walk with will end up influencing our destination. Who we spend time with matters, because our destiny is at stake. We will also play a part in determining theirs. No wonder Jesus went to a mountain to pray.

The blend

But Jesus wasn't just interested in choosing individuals. He was recruiting a team that would not only support him in his earthly ministry, but would also sit around the table of what was to become the world's most successful start-up. A lot depended on the group dynamic.

So far we have explored the friends who are closest to us. These are few in number. As the circles widen and numbers increase, Jesus gives us a fascinating example of what a diverse blend of relationships looks like. The encouragement of the next few pages is to pursue the same.

The line-up

As the coverage of a sporting event begins, the broadcaster gives an overview of the teams or individuals about to compete. Before we examine the dynamics of this group, here is a brief overview of the disciples and their backgrounds:

Peter Water-walking, three-time-denying, kingdom-key-holding fisherman from Bethsaida. After a rocky start (pun intended) he goes on to be the leader and spokesperson as the church explodes onto the scene after Pentecost.

James Least prominent of the inner circle, brother of John, son of Zebedee. Famous for wanting to call down fire on a Samaritan town. Perhaps appropriately named a 'Son of Thunder'. Fisherman, eventually killed by Herod (Acts 12:2).

John The previously discussed one who loved to write, the one Jesus loved. A powerful eyewitness of much of Jesus' activity. Fellow 'Son of Thunder', brother of James, fisherman and son of Zebedee.

Andrew Responsible for introducing his brother Peter to Jesus. His highlights reel includes sourcing the boy with five loaves and two fishes at the feeding of the 5,000. Another fisherman.

Philip Aside from having a great name, and a Greek name, Philip is from Bethsaida. He seems to have missed the point at both the feeding of the 5,000 and the Last Supper, with some silly comments, but does introduce some Greeks, as well as the next disciple to Jesus.

Bartholomew Also known as Nathaniel, introduced to Jesus by Philip. From Cana in Galilee – where Jesus turned water into wine.

Thomas Unfortunately also known as Didymus. (I'd have gone with 'Thomas' too.) Tees Jesus up for his world-famous line about being the way, the truth and the life, but the rest of his infamy is, perhaps unfairly, tied up in his doubt that Jesus has been resurrected.[4]

Matthew Also known as Levi (intriguing how many of them have an AKA), he is best known for his beautiful gospel account. Other notable interests: collecting taxes and holding banquets. Capernaum based.

James, son of Alphaeus We are now into those disciples we know least about. James, 'the less' as he is sometimes known, is only referred to in the gospels in the lists of disciples.

Simon the Zealot Member of a fearsome political sect that hated the Romans and wanted to overthrow the empire that was oppressing them.

Judas, son of James The lesser-known Judas, also known as Thaddeus. Makes one appearance outside the lists of disciples, asking Jesus a question at the Last Supper.

Judas Iscariot Before his notorious role, his one appearance is criticizing Mary's lavish worship of Jesus at Bethany. The rest – his betrayal, kiss and suicide – is history.

Quite a diverse and fascinating collection of followers! We will go on to explore their differences, but we must also reflect on one thing they had in common. Despite their obvious faults and limitations, which appear repeatedly in the story, they became part of something extraordinary. Jesus must have seen in them a passion for the things he was passionate about and a drive to see the world changed by his story. They were united by a desire to see God's kingdom come. Perhaps this appetite was even found in Judas, and his betrayal was motivated by a disillusionment with Jesus' methods and a misunderstanding of the way of the cross. This uniting passion, empowered by the Holy Spirit, resulted in the formation of the most powerful movement the world has ever known. What else do we notice?

Mates on a mission

The disciples were more Fellowship of the Ring than the assembled Avengers. Bear with me on this. Some collaborations are formed when a dream team of people are gathered for their specialist skills, with members never previously having encountered one another – like the Marvel team. Others mobilize from some former knowledge and relationship with one another – like Frodo's band of hobbits that added Legolas, Gimli and so on to their company.

My suspicion is that at least seven of the Twelve knew each other before Jesus called them.

Peter, Andrew, James and John were all fishermen on the Sea of Galilee. This was not a huge community, leading commentators to the conclusion that they 'had probably been lifelong companions'.[5] Philip was also from Bethsaida, the town of Peter and Andrew, meaning they probably went to the same synagogue. Philip clearly knew Bartholomew, and the fact that Thomas was included in their crew when they went fishing after Jesus' death suggests he was part of the trade as well. If this was the case it is likely that these seven men were friends before their lives were changed by meeting the rabbi from Nazareth.

Based on what we know about friendship, this should not be a surprise. The 'pillars' we need for that initial chemistry are important. These seven fishermen spoke the same language, were from the same place, had the same education and occupation, and held the same worldview and interests. But the next observation is critical.

Death stare

Have you ever been in a room with two people who want to kill each other? I have stood between two individuals desperate to inflict pain on one another. It is a toxic and intimidating place to be. And yet that may have been the mood music in the room when the disciples first met.

After the seven Galilean fishermen came a largely unknown five, but two names stand out. Matthew was a tax collector. This reveals a lot about him. The fiscal system imposed by the Roman Empire required three types of agent. The Gabbai were general tax collectors. They collected the official income and property tax. The Mokhes taxed trade. There were Great Mokhes, who worked behind the scenes (Zacchaeus was a Great Mokhes), and Little Mokhes, who worked in booths, taxing imports and exports as they passed down the road.[6] It was from one of these booths that Matthew was called (Matthew 9:9). The Mokhes in particular were universally despised. In essence, they had bought a tax franchise, could set their own rates and keep a percentage of their takings. They had sold out their national and religious identity for collusion with the Romans and a quick buck.

Simon was a Zealot. Under Roman occupation, different political parties took contrasting approaches to life under empire rule. Herod and the chief priests largely colluded with their masters, essentially sucking up to them to gain some delegated power. The Pharisees were the religious fundamentalists, believing that if the people would just stick to the rules they had created, God would redeem their situation. The Essenes decided to live as far away from empire rule as possible and so relocated to the desert. And then there were the Zealots. They wanted to kill Romans.

Zealots were freedom fighters – militant, violent outlaws who saw any kind of Roman sympathizer as a traitor. They had a small faction called the sicarii, or dagger men. These silent assassins carried small blades and would sneak up behind and execute Roman soldiers and statesmen. Oh . . . and tax collectors.

Imagine the first time Matthew and Simon went on a mission trip together. I hope Jesus made Simon leave his dagger behind.

Bonding and bridging

Political scientist Robert Putnam explains that we make connections in different ways. With some people we bond. Bonding involves forming deeper relationships with people we already have lots in common with. Peter would have bonded with Thomas. Bridging is more difficult and involves us making connections with people we have a lot less in common with. Matthew and Simon would have had some bridging to do. When it comes to crossing divides, Jesus was an architect of the finest relational bridges across the greatest of cultural canyons.

But what is wonderful about Jesus' huddle is that it required those in it to bond and bridge.

We need friends who are different from us.

We need them for our own benefit. Being part of the lives of people of different backgrounds, ages, ethnicities and worldviews deeply enriches our lives. Hearing a diverse range of perspectives and stories helps us appreciate the lives and experiences of people. The tapestry of society God has woven together is a beautiful blend of multicolour and multicultural threads. When we befriend only those who are like us we are choosing to live in monochrome. Bridging can push us out of our comfort zone, but the rewards are found in a greater love for the people God has made.

Close to home

Let me give you a personal example. Among other things, my dad was an incredibly successful lawyer, rising to be the senior partner at a large legal practice. He was compensated accordingly and I have no doubt that we could have lived in some sizeable properties. And yet he chose to buy a modest house in an area that ranks in the top 2% of economically deprived estates in England. Mum and Dad were criticized by friends for denying their children the best education, but not only did they believe they were doing what God had called them to do, the reward was also in the impact they had on our community and the beautiful friendships they made. Today we live on the next road.

Occasionally I will be in a conversation and someone will make an interesting comment about those living on benefits or from a background of poverty. When I dig a little deeper, these generalizations might be based on statistics they have read, but they rarely actually know someone from a community they are describing. If they were to spend time with some of my neighbours and hear their stories, my suspicion is that their judgements would soften.

Our street is deliciously diverse. I enjoy long conversations and laughs with my next-door neighbour, Pramod, who serves in the army and is training to be a nurse. Across the street live Tommy and Katie and their four wonderful daughters. A few years ago I invited Tommy to come on an Alpha course. All six of them are now significant members of our church and community. Next door to them lives Nask, who has found a home in the UK after having to flee her native country. She regularly blesses us with stunning plates of food, and her passion is caring for animals of all kinds. This has meant we have had escaped peacocks wandering down the road before a neighbour alerted Nask, who gathered them back up into her garden. Life is never dull.

They are not just neighbours; they are our friends, and our lives are richer for them.

For the sake of the world

A diverse group of connections is needed not just for our own benefit, but also for the sake of the very fabric of society. Our world faces many challenges today, and the fractures in our society and our inability to disagree well is making matters worse. Over half of people in the UK say that we are the most divided we have been as a nation. These fractures are deeply damaging to us as a society, and they are getting worse. Author Jon Yates explains and exposes the disunities that exist between those of different ages, races, incomes and political views.[7]

Age A study in the Netherlands found that in the average week, nine out of ten over-80s have no contact with anyone under the age of 60, apart from members of their own family.

Race In the USA almost half of white people have no black friends. A third of white Britons don't have any friends from an ethnic minority background.[8]

Income and education Almost a third of Americans with a college degree have no close friends without one.[9] A third of working-class Brits have no friends from a different social class. A European study across thirteen cities found that the middle classes were moving away from low-income neighbourhoods, and the poor were being forced out of desirable areas.[10]

Politics In the referendum on the UK leaving the European Union in 2016, a quarter of remain voters had no friends who voted leave. A fifth of leave voters had no remain voting friends.

And at the heart of these divisions is the simple truth that many of us don't know people who are different from us. Yates describes two forces at work in the world. First, there is our tendency to flock together with people with whom we share commonalities, something he calls 'People Like Me syndrome'. Second, is what he calls the 'common life', which encompasses the practices and cultures that bring us together across the various divides. In our world today, People Like Me syndrome is winning and the common life is in decline. It is a lot more difficult to hate a group of people if you are friends with someone from that group of people. The big problem at the moment is that we lack opportunity to rub shoulders and become friends with those who are different from us.

If most of your friends look like you, talk like you, have a similar education to you, think like you and vote like you, I understand. As we have seen, strong friendships begin when we find common ground with others. And for those closest to us, the strength of those relationships will be built on those commonalities. The fact that Peter, James and John had so much in common shows that this is to be celebrated. Our inner circle does not have to look like the United Nations. But as the circles extend, so should our diversity of friendship. Not only is it demonstrated in the Twelve, it is also good preparation for heaven. If we are to spend eternity with others from 'every nation, tribe, people and language', we should probably begin to get on with them now (Revelation 7:9).

For most of us, we are hopefully at least a few years away from joining the multitude in the heavenly city and before then we have the opportunity to embody the community of our future in the reality of the church. The antidote to the divisions in our society is the unity of the body of Christ. The fix for our fractures and flaws is found in the family of our Father. Jesus' prayer for us as his people is that we might be one (John 17:21). As a church we need to cling to the picture painted in Scripture of a church where every background, age, ethnicity and story is represented. For me, the best example of the 'common life' that Jon Yates describes as the remedy to the divisions in our world is the church.

Occasionally I've seen glimpses of this vision, and its beauty is staggering. I went to one church service in one of the poorest areas of the UK where on one side of me stood some men from the estate who had met Jesus, kicked their drug habits and had their lives transformed. On the other side of me stood some extraordinarily wealthy people. The stark differences in our stories and our bank accounts did not matter as we worshipped the God who had ransomed us all. On another occasion I was at a conference with people from all over the world. As we sang 'How great is our God', the worship leader lined up singers from tens of different countries, and one after another we heard the chorus in each language. It went on for some time, like some kind of Christian *Eurovision Song Contest*, but no-one was bored. The unity in diversity was captivating.

And it is a common faith that makes this unity possible. I have some friends in my huddle with whom I share very little in common, yet our strong friendship is formed on a like-minded passion for Jesus. In the situations I have described, despite the separations of circumstance and language, there has existed a deep connection between us. Tim Keller describes it like this:

> For believers in Christ despite enormous differences in class, temperament, culture, race, sensibility, and personal history, there is an underlying commonality that is more powerful than them all. This is not so much a 'thread' as an indestructible steel cable.[11]

Be a bridger

For almost all of us, bonding with people who are like us is more straightforward. It does not force us out of our comfort zone and the natural chemistry flows a lot easier. But the example of Jesus and the needs of the world urge us to be intentional in cultivating friendships with people who are different from us. There is power in listening to one another's stories and overcoming the awkwardness in crossing cultural bridges. We all long for acceptance. It is natural to feel insecure and fear rejection, and overcoming these fears is a significant step towards walking across the room to talk to someone who is different from you. But it is worth it, and I've seen the difference it makes.

The European migrant crisis in 2015 was a period of significantly increased movement of refugees into Europe. Some 1.3 million people sought asylum. At the time I was working for Youth for Christ, and we were supporting churches that were playing their beautiful part in welcoming migrants into their communities. In conversation with one church, the leader explained that the teenagers they were serving would love to go on a Christian camp that summer.

I have been part of a Christian water sports camp since I was 16. I contacted the leaders and explained the situation. They fired off an email asking for financial support to enable these young people to come along. Within hours the target had been exceeded and that August we welcomed ten refugees to Aquasports. It is safe to say that the teenagers who usually came to Aquasports had very little in common with the new group. On the first day there was a visible divide between the cohorts: the birds flocked together. Then a game of volleyball was suggested. At first, each group faced each other on different sides of the net. After a while, someone suggested mixing up the teams. By the end of the day friendships were forming.

A key moment came halfway through the week. During the evening entertainment, interviews often took place, where leaders would tell their story. One night we invited a couple of the Iranian teenagers to share their experiences. The usually boisterous audience was silent as a captivated marquee heard of an adventurous journey across Europe. Teenage bravado cracked and tears were seen running down the cheeks of the coolest kids on camp as their new friends told of families separated and reunited. Prejudices and stereotypes were replaced with compassion. By the party on the last night, every possible division had been destroyed as the group danced together with arms around each other, to both UK hits and Persia's finest chart anthems.

Bonding makes a difference to us, but bridging makes a difference to the world.

Group dynamic

So far we have focused on the diversity of the Twelve, but it is also worth celebrating their intimacy. It is clear from the gospels that these men spent a lot of time together. Amid the anxieties of being arrested by the Romans or stoned by the Pharisees, there must have been a great deal of joy. I imagine them gleefully recalling and describing the events of the day to each other, recollecting the thunderous sound of pigs rushing into the lake, the taste of Merlot from water jars, the sight of a man being lowered from a makeshift skylight, Peter describing the feeling of waves beneath his toes.

At times the joyful laughter must have been uncontrollable, and this image encapsulates what is so precious about these kinds of friendships. It is with those in your huddle, whom you know the best, that you are most likely to journey through the adventures of life and find yourself around a table or fireside, roaring with amusement. When I am asked to describe my perfect day, it always ends with a group of people I love the most sitting around burning embers with a glass of something tasty, laughing until I struggle to breathe. Laughter even plays a key role in helping us to bond, relaxing us around others and increasing levels of intimacy.[12]

One of the primary purposes of friendship is to share joy and celebrate the delights and trivialities of life. From crossing the Red Sea to the rebuilding of the walls of Jerusalem; from the finding of sheep and coins to announcing the resurrection, celebration is a team game. There is something electric and life-giving about huddling with good friends and treasuring each other's presence.

This is why Jesus picked a team. He understood our need for one another and the powerful dynamic that is kindled when a group of people huddle and interact. In our circles of approximately this size, our good friends may or may not know each other, but we need strong connections of this nature. Some will be like us; some should be very different. The time we invest in them is not quite what we give to our inner circle, but it is substantial and we can do so in groups of varying sizes. These groups provide the perfect environment for the magic of friendship to ignite.

The best of amends: top friendship tips

Walk across the room

When I hear the clattering of mugs at the end of a church service as hot drinks are prepared, I face the same weekly dilemma. Who do I chat with over my coffee? At my worst, I head for the safe haven of my friends who are my age, whom I have known for years, and with whom I can talk about yesterday's football. At my best, I seek out the people I've not met before, approach those who look different from me and talk to those significantly older or younger than me, as well as quickly catching up on the football! Here are a few questions I try to remember when I struggle to know what to say:

- What's been keeping you busy in the last week?
- What are you looking forward to in the next week or so?

- What's going well for you at the moment?
- What is a bit of a challenge?
- Is there anything I can pray about for you at the moment?

More often than not, the answers will lead to something interesting to be explored with a follow-up question: 'Tell me more about that . . .'

By being intentional about leaving our established crowd, we have a much better chance of building a more diverse circle of friends. This principle applies just as much at work or social gatherings as it does at the end of church!

Host and be hosted

Golden sessions rarely happen by accident. We need to be intentional about creating gatherings where we can interact and share the joys and sorrows of life. Here are a few things to consider:

- First make sure those at the top of the invite list can make it. When I organize a gathering, I set the date around the people I most want in the room and build from there. Consider who you might invite to combat People Like Me syndrome.
- Atmosphere matters. Think about where you will meet. If you are hosting, what is within your control? Consider lighting, the music and how you will welcome people. Do you want one big conversation or several smaller ones? How you arrange the seating will influence this.
- Ask yourself: will conversation flow naturally, or do I want to have a few questions up my sleeve to get people talking? Sometimes it is enough for people just to catch up on life and share a few funny stories. There may be other occasions where you deliberately encourage people to be vulnerable. As the host, you have the opportunity to encourage the direction of conversational travel.

Finally, you will not always be the host. Be as gracious in accepting invites as you are generous in extending them.

The themes of this chapter can be explored further using small-group resources, videos and discussion questions. Delve deeper at: www.philknox.co.uk

Further reading

N. Williams and P. Brown, *Invisible Divides* (SPCK, London, 2022). Natalie and Paul describe their journeys of becoming Christians from working-class backgrounds and ask whether our church cultures are designed to make us middle class as much as disciples of Jesus.

J. Yates, *Fractured* (HarperNorth, Manchester, 2021). A must-read for anyone interested in how to heal the divisions across our society.

7

Seventy-two – Jesus had a network

The single greatest 'people skill' is a highly developed and authentic interest in the other person.
(Bob Burg, 'The Single Greatest People Skill')

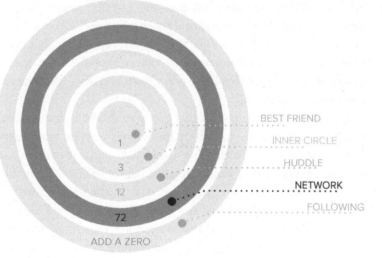

In the previous three chapters I have used a positive adjective to emphasize how close your friends need to be. You need a best friend, great friends and good friends. I have extolled the virtues of vulnerability. I have tried to persuade you to intensify intimacy with your closest friends. In this chapter I will try to do the opposite. You need friends who are 'just friends'.

Jesus' circles of relationships expanded wider than the Twelve. As we read the gospels, we stumble across many people with whom the Son of God seemingly met only once. We will examine these encounters in the next chapter. But there are others who land in this interesting 'no-man's-land' between his disciples and a one-off encounter. Exhibit A: the seventy-two.

Jesus' approach to influencing and making an impact was extraordinary. He did some of the work himself, but he also invested heavily in others, teaching them, modelling best practice and then sending them out to have a go themselves. As we have explored, the heaviest investment was in the Twelve, and Luke recalls this model of empowerment, where they were given 'power and authority to drive out all demons and to cure diseases' and then sent out 'to proclaim the kingdom of God and heal those who were ill' (Luke 9:1–2). But then, a chapter later, we see this pattern repeated with a wider crowd: 'After this the Lord appointed seventy-two others and sent them two by two ahead of him to every town and place where he was about to go' (Luke 10:1).

This is the only mention of this group in the Bible, but it's clear that Jesus knew those in this group moderately well. He was diligent and deliberative in selecting the Twelve. We must presume these appointments carried a similar relative degree of effort. Luke then tells us that when they were sent out, it was not a one-way missionary ticket; they 'returned with joy' and reported what they had seen and heard (Luke 10:17). We get the impression that Jesus' teaching journey was one of instruction, commission, return, report and reflection – probably in repetitive cycles, as their confidence and competence increased.

The seventy-two were not part of the huddle, but they were better relational connections than casual acquaintances. They were Jesus' network. They were 'just friends'.

There were more who met these criteria. The gospel writers paint a picture of Jesus' activities being surrounded by a travelling party.

Undoubtedly the number of these companions varied, sometimes limited to the Twelve but at other times swelling as people's encounters with Jesus had such an impact they found him irresistible and dropped everything to be part of his tribe for a period of time. We hear of one example of this in Luke 8. Jesus was travelling from village to village with his huddle, but also 'some women who had been cured of evil spirits and diseases'. Mary Magdalene, Joanna and Susanna are named, but there were 'many others', and their connection to Jesus was so strong that they were 'helping to support him out of their own means' (Luke 8:1–3).

Without access to Jesus' phone book or social media platform, we cannot add seventy-two to 'many others' to determine the size of Jesus' wider network, but I would put several denarii on its approximate size. My guess, based on the extraordinary correlation between Jesus' circles and modern social science so far, is that it was around 150.

One hundred and fifty

It turns out that 150 is to your network what 12 is to your huddle.

The average size of a Christmas card list is 154.

The average size of a wedding is 144.

The prediction of anthropologists and psychologists as to the limit of how many meaningful relationships we can maintain based on the size of our brain is 148.

As historians have estimated the size of villages, they have found a similar pattern. The Domesday Book, compiled by William the Conqueror in 1086, recorded the size of every community and conurbation in England. The average size was 150.

Some 700 years later, more census records asked if things had changed in seven centuries. The new average was 160.

I have the privilege of preaching on most Sundays of the year in a variety of different churches across almost every denomination:

rural and urban, charismatic and less so, centuries old and months new. I have spoken in churches with over a thousand members and in rooms where there were as many in the band as there were in the pews, but many would have a congregation size of about 150.

It seems like a really good guide, perhaps even ordained in the created order, to the limit of purposeful relationships we can maintain.

By the grace of God, we have enough emotional bandwidth to be friends with more than just our inner circles. We have an overflow of relational capacity to enjoy the friendship of a broad and beautiful variety of people of different ages and backgrounds – as well as those with whom we share huge amounts in common. But also, by the grace of God, we do not need to be *great* friends with all of them.

So what is this circle for? How do we maintain friendships within it without feeling as if we are holding back or compromising?

Take heart

In the early 1780s, William Wilberforce was a gifted young politician and socialite, but was not on track to make his mark on history. The trajectory of his life was radically readjusted by the presence of friends. The first friend of note was Isaac Milner. In 1784 they set off travelling together, touring southern Europe, and one of their main topics of discussion was faith. They read the New Testament together and as result Wilberforce became a passionate evangelical Christian.

With his newfound faith and a promising political career, he was hesitant about remaining in public life. At the same time he was bearing an increasingly heavy burden on his heart concerning the slave trade. Two more famous friends spoke game-changing words into his life. The first, John Newton, assured Wilberforce that his faith could be transformational in the spheres of influence in which he had been placed, writing to him, 'It is hoped and believed that the

Lord has raised you up for the good of His church and for the good of the nation.'[1] The second was Prime Minister William Pitt. In May 1787 he urged Wilberforce to bring proposals before Parliament to begin the end of the abhorrent trading of human beings: 'Do not lose time, or the ground will be occupied by another.'[2] The rest is history. On 25 March 1807 the Slave Trade Act was given royal assent.

Encouragement can change the world.

We all need the voices of hope and affirmation in our lives that call out the best in us and breathe life to our weary souls, fire to our aching hearts and steel to our fragile frames. These interventions cheer us on and cheer us up. They may not always lead to historic wrongs being righted, but in their own way they may save us from despair and ourselves. Many of these clapping hands and hollering cries come from our inner circles, but I have found that many more of these voices come from this wider group.

A significant role of this circle is mutual encouragement. We are all more fragile than we like to admit and when it comes to those who would speak reassurance and inspiration, we need all the help we can get.

One of my favourite people in the Bible is Barnabas. He is known as the son of encouragement. It is Barnabas who takes Paul under his wing in the early and embryonic stages of the former Christian-killer's faith. It is Barnabas who believes in John-Mark when others reject him. I aspire to 'be more Barnabas'.

To be the voice of encouragement in another's life is an underrated and underused virtue.

And the size and presence of those in the network matter. In a fascinating study, Rhoades and Stanley looked at the correlation between wedding size and stability of the marriage. First, it is no surprise that the number they selected to frame their report was 150, but the headline of their findings was that 'couples who had more than 150 guests at their ceremony had the greatest marital quality down the line'.[3] It seems the greater the size of your support and encouragement network, the more stable and secure your relationship will be.

During the Covid-19 pandemic, as I began to reflect on this notion of friendship in circles, I decided to write a list of those in my life I had been most grateful for in recent years and write a postcard to each person on it, expressing my thanks for their friendship and support. It was a small gesture that took just an afternoon of my time. The messages of thanks I received in reply were extraordinarily effusive.

Proverbs 16:24 puts it beautifully: 'Gracious words are a honeycomb, sweet to the soul and healing to the bones.' The things we say are powerful. Across the circles of friends, I want to urge you to use their power to build up those around you in a world where we find ourselves knocked down so often. At the heart of the word 'encourage' is the Latin for heart: *cor*. When we encourage, we speak heart, courage and strength into the core of another. Surround yourself with circles of friends who will do this for you and reciprocate with words of gratitude and grace.

Radiators and drains

My cycle ride from Land's End to John o' Groats took two weeks. Four of us braved wind, rain, sun and chafing. As you have got to know me through the pages of this book, I suspect you may have guessed that this author is one of life's optimists. To me the glass is always half full. On the 950-mile bike ride, my biggest battle was not against the steep inclines or the lactic acid building in my body; it was against becoming annoyed by the negativity of others when they began to moan. When you have a positive mindset, negativity can drive you crazy. I am also aware that if you have a more sober personality, too much relentless enthusiastic optimism can be equally irritating.

How does this relate to encouragement?

Some people are more 'Barnabas' than others. When we are around them our spirits lift and our anxieties dissipate. Time spent in their presence is life-giving. There are others who seem to suck the joy out of us. If they are behind us, grumbling about the weather while cycling the length of Great Britain, our pedals turn a little faster. My mum would articulate this in terms of radiators and drains.

It is easy to be in the presence of a radiator. These friends make us feel comfortable. They emanate warmth and good vibes. There are some friends' houses where I arrive and sink into their sofa. I immediately feel at home and my soul begins to recharge. These are my radiators.

Drains are not bad friends. They are not toxic or abusive in a way that means we should terminate the relationship – cut and run. But they are harder work. We have to put in more effort to oil the cogs of connection. We find ourselves as the radiator when we are with them and our emotional energy levels may be depleted after time spent together.

Whether someone is a radiator or a drain to you is entirely subjective. Some people are radiators to some friends and drains to others. We might know individuals who are incredibly life-giving to us at some times and emotionally exhausting at others. We may adopt these two postures, or aspects of them, at different times to different friends.

The important thing is that our network should contain radiators and drains. Of course, we all want to be surrounded by radiators all the time, but the gift of friendship is that we get to give it to those who need it most – and that is often those who may drain us. If all your circles contain only people who make you feel comfortable, it might be time to cultivate some connections with those you could be an exceptional blessing to. If you are surrounded by drains, you definitely need to find some radiators to be those vital voices of encouragement that refresh and renew your heart with each encounter. Ask yourself:

what is the radiator/drain balance like in my life at the moment? How can I be more of a radiator to those around me?

Friends to go paddling with

As we have explored, there is a great need in our world for more vulnerable relationships, honest conversations and friendships that plumb the depths of our fragile hearts. But there is significant benefit too in having some connections with whom our conversation spends most of its times in the warm shallow waters. We need friends to go paddling with.

Jesus did not and could not have maintained the same level of depth with his wider circle. Inviting the seventy-two up the mountain with him to meet Elijah and Moses may have increased his street cred, but his relationship with this layer would have most likely been limited to light conversation.

I have some people in my life whom I have known for decades. With some of this circle, I have gone deep on a handful of occasions, but 99% of our conversation is spent recalling hilarious shared memories, talking about events and people rather than ideas, and bantering and bartering over sporting trivia. In a life so hard pressed by intensities and pressures we all face, our friends bring welcome distractions and diversions. When I walk through grief, I need my inner circles to weep with. When I grapple with big questions, I need those who will listen and wrestle with me on deep matters. But I also want friends whose text messages have me reaching for the laughter emoji at the sight of their name.

Every court needs solemn advisors. It also needs a jester or two.

Laughter also plays a central part in helping us build more intimate relationships. If you want to bond a group of people, get them laughing together. It is seriously good for you, giving your torso a good muscular workout, while flooding your lungs with oxygen and your brain with endorphins. We laugh more when we are around others – the social dynamic multiplies its impact – and it relaxes us and causes us to feel more intimate with those around us.

One note of caution. Life's jesters also need friends who will go deep with them. There is a tragic litany of comedians who have brought such happiness to others and yet have themselves struggled with depression – the so-called 'sad clown paradox'. Those in your circles of friends who project the most joy in the shallows may well be struggling in the depths. Asking them how they are really doing from time to time is a worthwhile and honourable venture.

With a little help from my friends

My brother-in-law can fix almost anything. He mends cultures in companies, can build a computer from scratch and is the king of DIY. When Dani and I got engaged, he bought me my first tool bag and an 'Idiot's Guide to Do-It-Yourself'. I must admit, with great embarrassment, that it has not helped very much. I was, and still am, utterly terrible at household jobs. If you are ever in our home, take a look behind some strategically placed pictures to see the mess I have made on some of our walls! Fortunately, as well as my brother-in-law, I have friends who can stop things leaking, get engines running, find the important file I thought I'd deleted, and cover up the holes I have made.

Let's return momentarily to the women listed earlier from Luke 8, who supported Jesus financially. This list is fascinating as it contains Joanna, who was 'the wife of Chuza, the manager of Herod's household' (Luke 8:3). What I love about this is that we know Herod wasn't exactly a big fan of Jesus' activities – if you remember, he tried to have him killed as a baby. And yet here was someone significantly connected to his administration providing funds for Jesus' ministry.

The power of a network is that it connects us to others whom we can bless with the skills and resources available to us and be blessed by in return with expertise we can only dream of. Sociologist Mark Granovetter found that most of our relationships were, in his words, 'weak ties'. In our terms, these are the connections in this circle of friends. In 'The Strength of Weak Ties', he preaches their importance in gaining the information and help we need.[4] When I need a plumber, a plasterer, new music to listen to or a film recommendation, it's my network I turn to. Indeed, the book you are reading has many contributors who have helped its author by responding to questions about friendship posed on social media over the years of writing.

This is one of the beautiful things about belonging to a church family. We have the strongest thread running through us – a common pursuit of knowing Jesus – and yet we are diverse in so many ways, not least in our abilities to help one another out. So much business is generated for some of the tradespeople in our church, I am convinced that if I were a local handyman with no interest in faith, I'd join the local fellowship just for the business opportunities!

One of the challenges is that we do not like asking for help. Much of the damage to our house has been caused by my stubborn ambition to be independent. This desire is relentlessly reinforced by the individualistic narrative in our world. The truth is that we need each other, and sometimes great humility is required to ask for help. However, when we reach out and ask, it is not only good for developing our own character, it may strengthen our connection with those we reach out to.

This circle of 'weak ties' is worth investing in. Maintaining contact with a wide network of friends is of great value. You don't have to meet them for coffee every week, or buy them expensive birthday presents, but be interested in their lives, ask them how they are doing from time to time, provide them with encouragement and let them know you are thinking of them and praying for them occasionally. It is worth getting to know and meeting the breadth of the rich tapestry of characters and personalities God has created. Your network may be an overlooked source of blessing to you. It may also be a sphere in which you can offer something of infinite value.

Good news travels fast

Let me be clear from the outset. We do not make friends with people in order to convert them to Christianity. I hope these pages so far have convinced you that friendship for friendship's sake is not only of exquisite value, but also God's instruction, mandate and gift to us. Friendship evangelism has received some bad press in recent years and been accused of being inauthentic, manipulative and full of hidden agendas. Our primary motivation in making friends should always be that in doing so we are reflecting the image of the relational God and doing what we are created to do – to love our neighbour.

We become friends with those around us in the myriad of ways that friendship happens. And those we connect with will be at a variety of points on their journey of faith. In fact, in the spirit of diversity discussed in the previous chapter, we should invest in friendships with people at different stages.

I love my friends in all my circles who do not yet know Jesus. I can also honestly say that if I knew there was never any chance of them knowing him for themselves, I would not stop being their friend or devote any less energy or commitment to our friendship.

At the same time there is a happy tension that exists. Friendship is the vehicle through which most people make the most important decision of their lives, are invited into the one relationship they need the most, and can belong in the biggest and most beautiful family of them all. Research repeatedly reminds us of the role relationship plays in people choosing to follow Jesus. When Christians are asked who they credit with introducing them to the Christian faith, they repeatedly name friends, family members, colleagues and neighbours.[5] And yet many of us underestimate the vital role we all get to play in helping our friends on their journey.

First, we need to remember that we have in our hearts and our hands the greatest message of hope the world has ever known. Being a Christian is not comparable to a preference in football teams, a passion for your favourite restaurant or a captivating hobby. Choosing to follow Jesus is not like adding another new app to an already crowded home screen on your phone. He changes everything. When we turn our back on our old broken ways and put God at the centre of our lives, we receive forgiveness for our darkest past, his presence in our present and the most exciting hope for our future. This is why the most loving thing we can do for our friends is play our part in introducing them to the greatest Friend they could ever know.

Second, we constantly need reminding of the privilege and part we get to play in the lives of our friends. I am a missiologist, which means I am constantly researching and asking people how they came to encounter Jesus. As we have established, the research consistently points to friends playing a significant role, but I was fascinated to hear the stories of people who became Christians during the Covid-19 lockdown, when social distancing changed the way we interact. Surely the role of relationship would diminish, especially as online church exploded into life? What happened was intriguing. The internet did play a role, but the common denominator was still, you guessed it, relationship. The following story was typical.

As Covid restrictions arrived, 19-year-old Issy stumbled across some faith content on social media site TikTok. (If you don't know what that is or how it works, you are in the same boat as I am.) Next, she reached out to her Christian friend, who invited her to do an online Alpha course, at the end of which she decided to follow Jesus. She describes the change in her life:

> It's been such a U-turn. My perspective has changed. My outlook on life has changed. I'm happier. I feel more purpose. I've made friends. The people who knew the 'before' me

would never have expected it. My life has changed so much for the better.

Take a moment to imagine how it must have felt for Issy's friend who invited her to take the next step on the journey. You may be the only Christian in the circles of some of your friends' lives. If they are going to make the most important decision of their lives, the likelihood is that you will play a significant role.

I met others whose journey was remarkably similar to Issy's. All of them included the role of a Christian relational connection. Some of the relationships were representative of those in the inner circles, but for many, they featured in this wider network. How we prepare ourselves for moments like this is beyond the remit of this book, but you can read more in my previous work, *Story Bearer: How to share your faith with your friends*.[6] However, there are two important approaches I want to encourage you in. The first is about how we introduce people, the second is how we pray for them.

Connect your connections

One of my favourite things is introducing people to one another. With probably a bit too much pride, I like to look at longstanding friendships for which I was the catalyst.. Some great friends of ours went on to get married themselves after meeting at our wedding. When you have the opportunity to introduce people, do so with enthusiasm and generosity. Introduce others as you would want to be introduced. Unleash the superlatives and take the chance to big up your friends as you acquaint one friend with another.

You could say, 'Tom, this is my mate Rich. We work together.'

Or you could say, 'Tom, meet Rich. I have the utter privilege of sitting next to Rich at work. We share a mutual passion for football and the US version of *The Office*. He's an absolute legend.'

At this point, Rich is already more confident in engaging with Tom, and Tom's inner monologue is, *What is he going to say about me?!*

Make sure you don't just say, 'Rich, this is Tom. He's all right.' Make introductions count.

When thinking about how to help our not-yet-Christian friends take their next step on the journey of faith, an effective strategy is to find ways of introducing them to your Christian friends. This is especially important if we are the only Christian they know. First of all, it has enough merit on its own. When we create connections we reflect the divine: Jesus was constantly bringing people together. But it also helps those who do not yet know Jesus to encounter him in the lives of others.

Evangelist Sam Chan explains why this makes a difference. If you told some friends that you'd had an encounter with some extra-terrestrial beings, they may think you had lost your mind. However, if you told them this and then introduced them to some other friends who described a similar experience, they may begin to believe that your story was grounded in reality. To many of our not-yet-Christian friends, the idea of trusting your life to an executed rebel who lived 2,000 years ago is as extreme as a conviction that you were abducted by aliens. Meeting other credible, likeable, authentic people who also share a belief in Jesus builds plausibility structures for our unbelieving friends. It has an impact and helps them see that faith is reasonable and possible. Chan says: 'Here is the key idea you need to grasp: people will find a story more believable if more people in their community, their trusted friends and family, also believe the story.'[7]

It is common to have circles of friends slightly different from the ones we are describing in this book. We have work friends, school-run friends, church friends, sports-club friends – often all operating in complete isolation to one another. It can be more comfortable to keep these worlds apart, especially if we behave slightly differently within them. But the impact of bringing them together could be seismic. We can sensitively, winsomely and thoughtfully find the right moments and gatherings to bring our circles together, and in doing so we connect disconnected people and give those who don't yet know Jesus the opportunity to meet bearers of his story and the indescribable hope that he brings.

> Gradually, bit by bit, our universes will have both Christians and non-Christians, hopefully with a fifty-fifty split, and the Jesus story becomes more believable to our non-Christian friends because in a room of trusted friends, half the people believe in it.[8]

The home can be the perfect environment for this. When Dani and I got married and bought our first house, in a moment of frivolity we took a permanent marker pen and wrote our names on the wall in the hallway – perhaps a twenty-first-century equivalent of marking our territory. When we welcomed our first guests, we handed them the pen and they did the same. So it began. Fourteen years later and we have all but run out of wall space. (Our hallway is not that big!) Of the hundreds of names that represent our circles of friends, most of them would fit into this layer of relationship, and as well as providing a place of hospitality, we have connected people at every step on the journey of faith. Our friends who are far from God have seen and heard what a transformative relationship with Jesus looks like.

In *The Gospel Comes with a House Key*, Rosaria Butterfield models how radical hospitality has changed the lives of many in her circles of friends, but she also extols the virtues of making these kinds of introductions in her home: 'Have a house filled with God's people, who can then help our neighbours see the hand of God in the everyday details of life.'[9]

Food plays such an important role in helping us make friends. Perhaps one of the reasons we are facing a crisis in friendship is that we are eating together less. Just 28% of households in the UK share the same evening meal.[10] The amount of time friends spend eating together has decreased by 45% in the last thirty years.[11] When we gather around a table, we slow down, we face one another and join in a common, pleasurable activity. We enjoy a multisensory experience as we taste, listen, feel and smell together, and look one another in the eyes. The Bread of Life spent much of his time eating with his circles of friends. The rest of Scripture is bursting with meal times at momentous and mundane moments. It is no surprise some research finds that regularly eating meals alone is the biggest single contributor to unhappiness, besides mental illness.[12]

May we connect and cook and chew more together.

Praying in circles

There is a beautiful older lady in our church family called Janet. She has been faithfully praying for me for nearly thirty years. As I go into important meetings or get up to speak somewhere, I fire off a quick message to her asking her to pray. Janet, in turn, regularly asks me to pray for her. I actually see her very rarely, yet this connection has been vital to me over the years and has been maintained by an ongoing commitment to share the joys and sorrows of life together by praying for one another.

Do you have a Janet?

Ajith Fernando describes prayer as fuel to a Christian friendship: 'when we talk to God about one another we are strengthening the ties we have with each other'.[13] It is also something we can do to invest in the relationship regardless of geographical proximity. Many of those we pray for will be in our inner circles, and they should feature regularly in our prayer lives. I love that Jesus reassures Peter that he prays for him (Luke 22:32). This is one of the few insights into the content of his prayer life. But prayer is also a fantastic way of blessing and maintaining connection across our network. Jesus widens his parameters somewhat when he prays for the whole church in John 17.

Prayer across a network of friendship is widely encouraged in the early church. In eight of Paul's thirteen letters he asks the churches to pray for him. The book of Philippians exquisitely models the reciprocity of two parties assuring each other of their mutual backing in prayer. Paul thanks God every time he remembers them (Philippians 1:3) and prays that their 'love may abound more and more in knowledge and depth of insight' (1:9). At the same time he is a recipient of their intercession: 'for I know that through your prayers and God's provision of the Spirit of Jesus Christ what has happened to me will turn out for my deliverance' (1:19). The strength of the global church today, 2.2 billion strong and still growing, is built on the relationships of the communities in places like Corinth, Colossae and Philippi. Their relationships were catalysed by prayer.

If you are looking for more ways of strengthening your bonds with the 'weak ties' in this circle, my encouragement is to begin to pray for them. Let them know you are praying and ask them what you can be praying for. Commit to doing so on a regular basis. I don't know how it works, but I know I have been sustained and inspired in inexplicable ways by the prayers of others. And the aforementioned William Wilberforce? History recounts that he suffered terrible migraines and immense internal and external pressure. A profound source of energy and encouragement for him came from a group of his friends, the Clapham Sect, who prayed passionately for him and rallied together a small army of praying voices from across the nation. Each of these intercessors also played his or her part in the eventual freedom of thousands of slaves.

Finally, don't forget to include not-yet-Christian friends on your list of people to pray for. Prayer is a crucial ingredient in the mix of how our friends come to faith in Jesus. When my first book, *Story Bearer*, was published, with no parental pressure my son Caleb insisted that it become part of his bedtime reading. One of the suggestions the book makes is to start a list of people to pray for to become Christians. Caleb, aged 9, I think in part to delay his bedtime, began to pray each night for his whole class to become Christians.

One day he returned from school exceptionally excited (I don't know where he gets that from).

'Daddy!' he exclaimed. 'Something really amazing happened today. Bradley became a Christian.'

I was so thrilled for him. 'Wow!' I said. 'Tell me what happened.'

'Well,' Caleb began, 'I went up to Bradley and said, "Bradley, do you want to live for ever?" Bradley said, "Yes." I said, "Well, you've got to become a Christian then." Bradley said, "Okay." I said, "You're now a Christian." Bradley said, "Great."'

A few points of clarification are needed here. First, that is not the approach recommended in *Story Bearer*. Caleb and I will be rereading it together soon. Second, if his evangelistic approach is like that when he is 29, we may need to rethink how we communicate the good news. But as Caleb's dad I was so encouraged by three things.

First, I think we could all do with some of that boldness when talking to our friends about faith. I so often bottle it in conversations with friends and have missed countless opportunities over the years.

Second, it shows the unequivocal hope in Caleb's heart that he has in Jesus. Being reconciled to God really is a matter of life and death, and as his dad one of the things I pray for most is that my sons know that hope for themselves.

Third, it demonstrates what happens when we pray. I cannot explain how it works, but somehow our prayers make a difference to those we pray for and help them on the journey of faith. They also inspire us to make the most of the opportunities we have, to live out and share the hope in our hearts.

A more thorough explanation of the link between friendship, evangelism and prayer can be found in *Story Bearer*, along with a more relational approach to sharing your faith than my son's aggressive line of questioning.

I hope you feel deeply encouraged by this book to prioritize friendships for lots of reasons, but let this one sink in. The power of relationship doesn't just help *us* live longer; it has an impact on the eternal lifespan of our friends. When Christians were asked to share their main barrier to sharing faith, the most common reason was 'a lack of significant relationships with people who aren't Christians'.[14] Don't cultivate connections with the sole agenda of converting them, but do prayerfully and intentionally invest in your relationships with not-yet-Christians in the hope that they might come to know the way, the truth and the life.

As we have explored this circle, some readers will have identified that while they have a few friends in their inner circles, this one could do with some strengthening. Others will have recognized they have a wide network of connections and will have been encouraged to deepen the relationship with some and by doing so invite them into a closer relationship. This balance is an important one, but there is plenty of margin for error and we are all created differently, with different needs, personalities and opportunities. No-one has the exact numbers of friends described here, but I hope they have been a useful guide as we have examined them and their significance over the last few chapters.

Introverts beware: it's time to add a zero. In the next chapter we will open the circles to their widest possible reach.

The best of amends: top friendship tips

How do we develop this circle? How do we maintain enough contact with those in our various networks?

The table

My wife Dani is an expert connector. Interestingly, she would say that she hasn't always been this way. She has deliberately tried to invest in herself to improve her relational skills and exercise her hospitality muscles. Because my job means that I am almost always preaching at another church on a Sunday morning, she felt inspired to give herself some company. She wrote out a list of everyone in our church family and one by one began to invite them over for lunch on a Sunday. (They also got to write on the wall in our hallway!)

We can just about get eight people around our kitchen table and she considered the dynamic carefully, thinking about those who knew each other already and, crucially, those who didn't. Each Sunday she cooked the same simple meal and watched the relational magic happen. People who had been part of the same church for years but had rarely spoken to one another ate, shared and laughed together. In one year of Sundays, Dani fed and connected well over 100 people. She said that the most rewarding thing of all was watching people who had not connected before becoming friends and observing them giggling over coffee the following Sunday at church.

Imagine if a few people in your church began to do this. Imagine what would happen to the strength of the relational bonds in your church family. If you are a church leader, how could you facilitate and encourage more meals like this? Author Wes Hill observes, 'Priests and pastors have a vested interest in their congregations being filled with people who are friends with one another.'[15] It is said that people come to church for many reasons, but they stay because of one: relationship. You don't need to cook a Michelin-star meal; soup and a roll will suffice. So grab a pen and paper and begin your first invite list now.

RSVP

Recently I received an invitation to a birthday party from someone who is some distance from my inner circles. He is 'just a friend'. We haven't got many mutual friends and the instinctive thought that I might be left awkwardly hanging around with no-one to talk to led me to begin to draft the reply to the invitation with an apology and a 'Happy Birthday'.

But instead, I reconsidered. I decided it would be an encouragement to my friend for me to be there and a good opportunity to get to know some new people. It turned out to be a brilliant evening and I headed home with heart enlivened by good conversation and a few more connections in my wider network.

We cannot say yes to every invitation, but our addiction to being emotionally comfortable means that we often say no to those that would grow or encourage our friends in this circle, because we are afraid to step out of our comfort zone. Next time you get an offer to meet some new people or hang out with someone in your network, why not say yes and see what happens?

Insta-couragement

Earlier in the book, we considered how social media can be detrimental to our relationships, but it also has immense value in enhancing our connections, especially with regard to our network. First, when you meet for the first time, an 'add friend' or a 'follow' on social media can be an easy, less intrusive way of sharing contact details and letting people know you want them in your circle. Sow and Friedman explain:

> There's a reason adding each other on your social platform of choice has become an important step at the beginning of a friendship. After you've met and felt that spark, but before you've put in the hours and gotten truly vulnerable, adding or following someone can carry the weight of intention. You want them in your feed, you want them in your life.[16]

Second, the variety of technological tools we have at our disposal means it has never been easier to send notes of encouragement to those in our network. What if for every metre of 'death scrolling' down our social media feeds we sent a note checking in on a friend, asking them how they are doing, taking a moment to pray for them and asking if there is anything specific they need prayer for? When I consider the distances of newsfeeds I get through with my thumbs, that's a lot of encouragement.

Open circles

The final top tip in this area concerns physical circles of friends. When we gather at parties, at the end of church or in business settings, it can feel natural to 'close off' the circle when we stand or sit together. This makes it very difficult for someone to join in, especially if they don't know anyone and are looking for opportunities to make a connection. When you find yourself in these physical circles, take a small step back and turn your body a few degrees to open the circle, ready to welcome someone else to the conversation.

When someone new arrives, welcome them, introduce yourself and ask, 'What keeps you busy when you are not here today?'

The themes of this chapter can be explored further using small-group resources, videos and discussion questions. Delve deeper at: www.philknox.co.uk

Further reading

R. Butterfield, *The Gospel Comes with a House Key* (Crossway, Wheaton IL, 2018). This is a beautiful and challenging book about opening our homes and practising hospitality.

S. Chan, *Evangelism in a Skeptical World* (Zondervan, Grand Rapids MI, 2018). Full of creative ideas and cultural insight to help us share faith naturally and effectively.

P. Knox, *Story Bearer: How to share your faith with your friends* (IVP, London, 2020). In my first book, I aim to help you tell your story and live your life in a way that helps others become Christians.

Download the i61 app from the app store for an interactive journey to help you share life, share faith and share Jesus with your friends.

8

Add a zero –
Jesus had a following

No act of kindness, no matter how small, is ever wasted.
(Aesop)

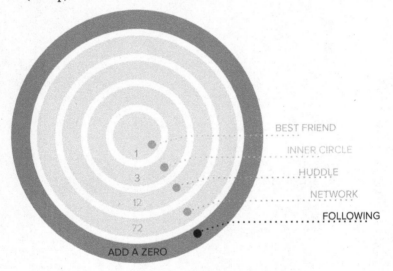

Growing up, our family would spend three weeks each summer holidaying on the Isle of Islay, a Hebridean island off the west coast of Scotland. To get there meant an annual pilgrimage involving endless motorways, games of 'I spy' and choruses of 'Are we there yet?' The mood in the car changed, along with the scenery, just north of Glasgow, when we crossed the River Clyde and knew that our destination was getting closer. To add to the excitement in the back of the car, we drove across the river on the magnificent Erskine

Bridge, and to do so meant paying a toll at the booth. At this point, my dad would invariably do something that would cause some passengers in the car to cringe with embarrassment and others to whoop joyfully with delight: he would pay not only for our crossing, but also for that of the unwitting car behind. As we pulled away, I would watch giddily through the rear window as the next vehicle approached to be told that their fare had been paid by the gentleman in front. I still remember the looks of surprise and delight on strangers' faces at this small gesture of generosity as we sped off over the bridge.

Small acts of kindness can make another's day.

There are 7.7 billion people on planet earth. We will not even meet most of them, let alone have the opportunity to form meaningful relationships with them. But most of us will interact with thousands of people during our lifetime. This is a chapter about the biggest possible circle of relationships in your life, the people you will only ever meet once, the fleeting encounters, the countless momentary connections that are justifiably forgettable. When the end credits roll on the screenplay of your life, these are the last names to appear, under the heading 'Extras'.

The sheer number of people on planet earth is an overwhelming concept. That's why this framework of circles is a helpful reminder that we don't need to treat each connection with the same intensity of time or emotion. But lives can be changed in one-off encounters and here we are going to explore two different types of engagement in this circle and ask how we make the most of these interactions.

The power of the smallest gesture

The first is the briefest of moments of human contact: the person we pass in the street on the school run, the barista we buy our coffee from, the colleague we pass in the corridor. These moments are so frequent as to appear inconsequential, but they matter.

A friend of mine once took me out to dinner and told me how he had been walking in a park recently and seen a family acquaintance he didn't know particularly well, who was also out for a stroll. My friend was having an especially good day, so addressed this person with a cheery 'Hey! How are you doing? Lovely to see you!' That was the full extent of the 'conversation'. The acquaintance merely smiled back awkwardly. Weeks later, my friend had found out that the person had been contemplating taking their own life and as a direct result of that smile and greeting had had a rethink. 'I barely remember seeing this acquaintance,' he told me, with tears in his eyes.

The smallest gestures can have the biggest impact.

There is power in looking someone in the eye and smiling at them. That minuscule piece of non-verbal communication can change a person's day. I remember at the peak of the Covid-19 pandemic, when lockdown restrictions were at their greatest, being out for my one permitted walk of the day and smiling at people as I passed them on the street. As relational creatures starved of human interaction, we were all ravenous for moments of human contact at that time. As a result, more than ever, my fellow daily exercisers beamed back at me and were extraordinarily emphatic with their 'Good morning!'

Eye contact is particularly important when considering the homeless person we pass on our commute. It's unrealistic to stop and get to know everyone sitting on the side of the street, but meeting someone's gaze, smiling and saying 'Hi' or 'God bless you', makes that person feel less invisible. Just because people are visible doesn't make them feel noticed. I can be so tempted to stare intently at my phone as I walk by, afraid that I will feel challenged to engage with them or buy them a sandwich. At my best, a coffee gets bought, a name gets learned and a prayer gets prayed. At my worst, I'm embarrassed to say that I pretend an important text has just been received and I look away. The least we can all do is make eye contact and smile. I can't imagine Jesus deliberately looking away.

But smiling and nodding isn't the only type of one-off encounter we have. Sometimes, for just a few minutes, our story finds an intersection with another's, and two strangers make themselves known to one another. The vast majority of us don't go out of our way to make this happen and social norms mean that we are extremely wary of people who strike up conversations on public transport or approach us in the street. But occasionally we find ourselves in situations where we need help from or can offer help to a stranger and a conversation begins.

The deeper encounter

It is fascinating that in the accounts we read of Jesus, despite most of his time clearly being spent with his innermost circles of friends, some of his most memorable encounters were with people who only met him on one occasion. Because of the comparative brevity of Jesus' ministry, shortened further by at least 3,000 miles on the road (not to mention forty days in the wilderness!), it is unlikely that these one-off meetings with people he healed, conversed with or drove demons out of were the subject of follow-up visits.

There are a couple of things we can learn from the way Jesus treated these one-off encounters that may help us as we consider our own interactions with strangers.

Reactive and proactive

First, the response of Jesus to strangers was both reactive and proactive. Many of the stories in the gospels begin with the approach of an individual to Jesus with a request or a question.

- 'My daughter has just died. But come and put your hand on her, and she will live' (Matthew 9:18).
- 'Lord, if you are willing, you can make me clean' (Matthew 8:2).
- 'Good Teacher, what must I do to inherit eternal life?' (Mark 10:17).

- 'Jesus, Son of David, have mercy on me!' (Luke 18:38).
- 'Rabbi, who sinned, this man or his parents, that he was born blind?' (John 9:1)

In the situations above, these men and women were the instigators. Jesus was simply available, approachable and responsive. I wonder how often our busy twenty-first-century lives, our lack of margin in our daily planners, our headphones-in/eyes-on-screen postures and personas prevent us being available, approachable and responsive.

It's also a beautiful characteristic of Jesus that in a couple of the interactions above he didn't just perform his service and move on as quickly as possible, but responded with a question, prolonging the encounter and inviting deeper conversation. He asked the rich young man, 'Why do you call me good?', beginning a dialogue that drove at the heart of the man's desires. With Bartimaeus, we can reasonably presume that Jesus would have known what was needed for the blind man from the outset. Nevertheless, he wanted to talk, asking, 'What do you want me to do for you?' Had Jesus merely waved his miraculous hands without breaking stride, perhaps the healed Bartimaeus would have stayed where he was and not followed his healer along the road. It seems to me Jesus cared as much about the means as the end in these reactive situations. The rendezvous mattered as much as the result.

But Jesus didn't just let one-off encounters happen to him. On several occasions he became the intentional instigator, seeking out divine appointments to change the trajectory of someone's life. On a journey through Samaria, he sat by a well, tired, until a Samaritan woman appeared. If a small hammer is required to break the ice to begin a conversation between strangers on the London Underground, the iceberg between Jesus and this woman required a heatwave. In beginning a conversation, he was breaking down racial, cultural, religious and gender barriers.

Racially and culturally, Samaria was the place of outlaws and outcasts.[1] The Jews had a religious prayer, 'May I never set eyes on a Samaritan.'[2]

In gender terms, in the first century most upright Jewish men did not speak to women in public, not even relatives. A second-century Jewish scholar, Rabbi Eliezer ben Hyrcanus, expressed a common opinion in Jesus' day: 'The words of the Torah should be burned rather than entrusted to women.'[3] Many would have joined in the morning blessing, which included the line, 'Blessed are you, Lord our God, Ruler of the Universe, who has not made me a woman.'[4]

If you needed an example to follow of a God who delights in breaking down the superficial divisions we construct around us as his children, this is a pretty good example. And in contrast to the young ruler, Bartimaeus and other truth- or healing-seekers, it was a proactive engagement on Jesus' part; he actively wanted to converse with the woman and invite her to change her mind about who he was and take positive steps on her journey of faith.

Sometimes God actively leads us to disrupt the lives of strangers.

Zacchaeus is another example of Jesus taking the initiative in reaching out. The distinction with the short tax collector is that he seemed to be already interested in Jesus and, as recreated in millions of Sunday school craft activities, climbed a tree to see him. Jesus noticed him, knew his name, drew him down from the tree, ate with him, turned his life around and declared that salvation had come to his house.

Sometimes God actively invites us to play a one-off part in the journey of someone seeking him.

Positive and negative outcomes

The second thing we can learn from Jesus' one-time encounters is that the impact on the stranger varies dramatically. Even for the Son of God, there was not always a positive outcome. Some of the saddest words in the gospels tell us that in response to the invitation of Jesus to sell his possessions and follow him, 'the man's face fell. He went away sad, because he had great wealth' (Mark 10:22). My suspicion is that the rich man wasn't the only one who went away from that encounter sad. Jesus looked at him and loved him and would undoubtedly have felt a greater ache and wrenching of his heart as he watched him leave. As we consider our own interactions with strangers, we can take heart from the knowledge that when they end with a tinge of regret or the taste of disappointment, we are in good company.

That said, as we read the accounts of Jesus' life, we are more often left reflecting that his reactive and proactive meetings with tax collectors, promiscuous Samaritans, lepers, Roman soldiers, bleeding women and blind beggars went quite well. Most of them would use words like 'game-changing' or 'life-defining' to rightly describe meeting Jesus. There were many more whose paths crossed the light of the world just once and whose darkness was swept away.

The rest of Scripture is full of all kinds of encounters that shaped destinies, not just of individuals but of whole nations. Abram's meal with Melchizedek and the blessing he receives in Genesis 14 plays its part in setting the trajectory of the father of the Jewish nation. Philip's conversation with the Ethiopian eunuch in Acts 8 results in his conversion and him returning home to be the first person we know of to take the good news to Africa. From this conversation the gospel reached that great continent for the first time. Today there are 631 million Christians in African nations.

My one-off encounters: the good, the bad and the ugly

People who know me a little think I love talking to strangers. My extroversion is often interpreted as a source of boundless confidence. The truth is I am more than reluctant. But over the years I have become better at being receptive when I've needed to be reactive, and being obedient and sensitive when I have felt God challenge me to be proactive. As you will see, I have experienced the highs, lows and everything in between as I have nervously and tentatively engaged with those in my outermost circle.

It was a Sunday night and I was in the pub to watch football with a friend. I went to the bar to buy some drinks and met Steve. Steve had been drinking most of the day and after some pleasantries he told me he was a comedian and into marketing. He then asked what I did for a living. I wasn't sure he would have heard of the largest and oldest movement of evangelicals (I had just started working for the Evangelical Alliance), so I simplified things for both of us and told him I worked for the church. Here's how the exchange panned out:

'So you're religious then?'

I paused, not the greatest fan of that label. 'I wouldn't describe it as religious, Steve. I would say I'm a Christian, I'm a follower of Jesus. It's about a relationship with God.'

'So you're religious then?'

I decided not to fight this one any further, and put the white flag out. 'Yes, Steve, I'm religious.'

'I'm not religious. No . . .'

I tried to look accepting and reassuring, while still trying to catch the eye of the barman, who at some point took my order before Steve continued.

'But I like to believe there's something, you know, for those you love.'

Definitely ready to return to my thirsty mate, thinking that I probably would never see Steve again, and unsure that he would ever remember the conversation, I plucked up the courage to go for it and try to communicate the good news to this searching soul.

'Steve,' I began, smiling kindly, 'I really do believe that there is something, and not just for your loved ones, but for you. God loves you. He wants to know you and he has plans for your life.'

It is at these moments I dream of people like Steve welling up with tears, perhaps even falling to the ground and asking, 'What must

I do to be saved?' This story didn't end like that. He mirrored my smile, but replied with two colourful words that are unrepeatable in this context, telling me where I could shove my good news. I can take comfort in the fact that I am sure Jesus probably got the Aramaic equivalent at times. One-off encounters don't always result in the transformation of a continent. Sometimes they don't even result in the transformation of a single person.

Another memorable moment of bravery happened during Lent a few years ago. As a church we were meeting each morning at 6:30 a.m. to pray, and each day I would pass the same man at the bus stop, having woken up just minutes before for my daily dawn sacrificial pilgrimage. After a few days I felt God nudge me to offer to pray for this man who, for whatever reason, often looked a little sad (he may have just not been a morning person). I resisted the nudge for a few days and tried to make the same excuses to God before plucking up the courage to say something.

'Hi mate,' I said nervously. 'I've been passing you each day and I felt like God wanted to let you know that he loves you and I wondered if there was anything I could pray for for you today?'

Again I waited, perhaps expecting him, in an unforgettable moment, to burst into tears and tell me he'd been longing to hear someone tell him that all his life. He didn't and simply replied with these words that I will admittedly not forget, but for the wrong reasons: 'I'm sorry, I don't speak English.'

At that point, the bus arrived and that was that. I could almost hear the laughter in heaven.

But in those moments I also sensed the smile of God. Sometimes, when we step out in the ways I have described, they are more for our benefit than the other person's. When the red face of mild humiliation replaces the champagne moment of celebration, we learn not to take ourselves too seriously. It is in the moments outside the comfort zone, where we step out in obedience – whatever the results – that God does a work *in* us, even if there seems to be a perceived lack of results of his work *through* us. These adventures are sometimes more about the journey than the destination.

Author Robin Gamble observes this of evangelists:

Despite what everyone seems to think, evangelists are not the ones who find it easy, they do not have an endless supply of inner boldness; they are simply the ones that do it, and the more they do it, the better at it they become.[5]

And in my experience, the positive encounters far outweigh the negative. I have forgotten the many names of the taxi drivers I have chatted to, homeless men and women I have bought coffee for, strangers I have prayed with in the street, but these countless one-off meetings almost always leave me with a sweet rather than bitter taste in the mouth.

When Covid-19 struck, I struggled with the isolation that came with the lockdown regulations. I was also working from home and finding it hard to resist popping into the kitchen for a snack at regular intervals. The consequence of these two factors meant I decided to run more, and as I did, I occasionally felt God prompting me to stop and pray for people I passed.

The first encounter was with a guy called Stevie. The words tripped awkwardly out of my mouth as I mumbled something about being a Christian and wondering if I could pray for him. Despite my fears and inadequacies, he was blown away that I would stop and take the time to talk to him. Since that first meeting, we have seen each other a few times and got to know each other. Stevie is a former Amateur Boxing Association champion and soldier with a fascinating story.

I've now lost count of the number of people I've prayed with on the streets around where I live. I've prayed for and shared a burger with Kyle, just out of prison and making a fresh start. Harrison and I stood together and gave thanks for his newborn son. I prayed for James's mum and asked for strength for him to escape his addiction to illegal substances. I blessed a whole family on the way to their first day back at school.

And as the encounters keep coming, I'm learning a couple of things . . .

First, people are far more open than you would think. The gratitude of the prayed-for has far exceeded the faith of the prayer-bringer. One of my favourite moments came as I prayed for Max and Rhea. It was 7:30 in the morning. Max was already swigging from a can of lager. He was so thankful for my prayer he prayed one in return. I'm not sure he'd ever prayed before and what came out of his mouth was hardly from the Book of Common Prayer, but it was beautiful in the Lord's ears. Only one person has ever said no.

Second, being ready with some of what you are going to say makes people feel comfortable and you feel confident as you approach them. My line is, 'I'm sorry to bother you. I'm a Christian, and as I run/walk I pray for people and I felt God wanted me to pray for you today. Is there anything I can pray for for you?' Being aware of your surroundings and your safety is also paramount. I have not offered to pray with a woman on her own. I have not approached anyone at night.

Some people I will never see again; some have become friends. I was out running with a mate of mine when we met Mick. He was bent over in agony with a bad back and was more than two miles from his flat. We prayed for him and then helped him back home. Since then, we have helped him with some jobs, got to know him and seen him regularly. We often talk about Jesus together.

Sometimes the one-off encounters turn into lifelong friendships. Sometimes someone we meet in the outermost circle of friendships makes his or her way through the rings to the centre of our life. But we need to make peace with the fact that most of the time we will never be known by or know too much about the lives of those whose stories we intersect with only for a moment. This is a good thing. We would be overwhelmed if we had to make space in our inner circles for every person we interacted with. As Malcolm Gladwell observes,

'Sometimes the best conversations between strangers allow the stranger to remain a stranger.'[6]

But that doesn't mean we should always ignore or avoid them. With every person we meet, we have the opportunity to bring light and life to his or her day, even for a moment. With some, we may sense the nudge to engage a little deeper, to react or proactively engage in conversation and even sense where God is at work. A few in this circle may edge closer to our core friendships, but they will be the exceptions rather than the rule.

Jesus understood this. As we have seen, he masterfully fostered the circles of friendship that surrounded him, creating space to grow the deepest of friendships with his innermost orbits, while never underestimating the power of a conversation with or act of generosity to someone he would only ever meet once. May we follow his example. From a smile in the street to a random act of toll-bridge kindness, from a gracious response to a request for help to offering a prayer to a stranger, may we always appreciate the potential of God using us to impact our outermost sphere of influence.

Jesus had a following.

Exercise – draw your circles

As we have journeyed from 'best friend' to 'following' through the layers of 'inner circle', 'huddle' and 'network', you have presumably been reflecting on your own relationships and asking yourself which friends fit where in each of my circles. This is a good stage to pause and map out your current landscape of relationships.

Take a piece of paper and draw out the familiar concentric circles shown in Figure 3 on page 142. Begin to think about the people in your life. As an aide-memoire, you might like to scroll through the contacts in your phone. Populate the circles with the names of those who fit in the various layers. As you do, give thanks for them.

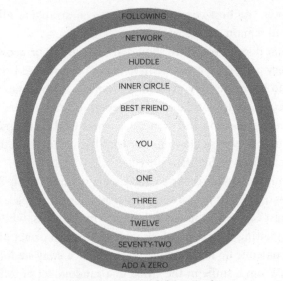

FOLLOWING

NETWORK

HUDDLE

INNER CIRCLE

BEST FRIEND

YOU

ONE

THREE

TWELVE

SEVENTY-TWO

ADD A ZERO

Figure 3 **Friendship circle**

When you have done this, take a look at how many names are in each circle. How close are the numbers to those in Jesus' circles? Which layers feel a little full? Where are there some gaps?

Next, prayerfully consider the names in front of you. Give thanks for each as your eyes pass over it. Then consider if they are all in the right circle. There may be some in front of you whom you would really like to get to know better. Draw an arrow next to these towards the centre of the circle, into the layer you would like them to be in. Think carefully, especially about your inner circles, particularly if these areas are not as populated as you would like.

Then there may be names of those in the inner three circles whom you feel you need to be less intentional with. If you have double figures of people who regard you as their best friend, it's probably time to create some relational bandwidth for the sake of all of your relationships. You may also have drawn a few arrows into these circles and need to create some room. With these friends, draw an arrow away from the centre of the circle to the appropriate layer. This will feel difficult, harsh even, but you are not cancelling the friendship; you are creating emotional capacity to invest more wisely and fruitfully in other friendships.

Next, write a list of the friends with arrows next to their name and, using all of the practical tips in the book so far, consider how you might be intentional about developing those relationships that need intensifying and how you might sensitively and gradually begin to decrease the energy and time you invest in the friendships that need less of your attention.

Finally, don't get too caught up with the exact numbers. They are the perfect guide, but friendship is a dynamic, relational dance rather than the organizational chart of a company. At any given time we will have some friendships that have been mainstays of our circles for many years, as well as others moving in and out through the layers. This will be particularly true if our life circumstances have changed with a house move, new job or relationship breakdown. The purpose of the exercise is to get a snapshot of the current state of your relational health and be intentional about who to invest your relational energy in.

The themes of this chapter can be explored further using small-group resources, videos and discussion questions. Delve deeper at: www.philknox.co.uk

Further reading

M. Gladwell, *Talking to Strangers* (Penguin, London, 2020).
Fascinating, captivating and powerful storytelling and research about how we relate to one another and how we form first impressions.

G. Jones, *The Peg and the Pumice Stone* (Instant Apostle, Watford, 2019). Fun and moving book packed with stories about how to connect with people well and share the good news of Jesus.

9

× (multiply) – Moses had a mentor . . . and an apprentice

In the Knox household, there is a Christmas tradition almost as sacred as present-opening, carols and singing Happy Birthday to Jesus on the morning of 25 December. On the day when work and school are over for the year, we watch *Home Alone*. I am so familiar with these 103 minutes that:

- I can tell you the exact address of the McCallister residence;
- I can sing you through the exquisite John Williams soundtrack;
- I annually mouth my way through the pizza delivery scene, telling him to keep the change.

I still laugh as Harry and Marv are assaulted by blow torches, nails, Micro Machines, paint tins and Buzz's tarantula, but what moves me most with each viewing is the narratives of reconciliation that accompany the physical torture of burglars. Kevin's forgiveness of his family pivots around an encounter he has with Old Man Marley, a bearded snow shoveller who, in turn, is reunited with his estranged son after the encouragement of 8-year-old Kevin. The unlikely friendship between old and young is a beautiful feature of the film in an age when birds of the same age group flock together.

For the next leg of our friendship journey, we are going to rewind a further thousand years and look at three types of relationship modelled and embodied by another biblical hero. Moses was connected to his forefathers, invested in his successors and dedicated to his Creator. We will deal with these in turn.

One of the features of this book has been to identify the threats to our connections and highlight some of the divisions in our society. Some divides are more obvious than others. One that often goes unnoticed is the erosion of relationship between the generations.

Creaking joints

One cultural commentator expressed his frustrations with the younger generations like this: 'What is happening to our young people? They disrespect their elders, they disobey their parents. They ignore the law. They riot in the streets, inflamed with wild notions. Their morals are decaying. What is to become of them?'

These words seem at home in the twenty-first century, but they were actually written by Plato in the fourth century BC. Peter the Hermit similarly lamented in 1274: 'The young people of today think of nothing but themselves. They have no reverence for parents or old age.'

It seems this is not a new problem. But it is a real and current one.

Fissures and cracks cover the intergenerational landscape of the UK. We have seen them play out in the news stories of recent years. After the Brexit vote, some younger generations blamed older generations for 'stealing their future' after the EU referendum.[1] During the Covid-19 restrictions, young people were accused by their elders of recklessly breaking rules, causing a rise in infection rates.

Half of young and middle-aged adults say that they do not have a single friend over 70,[2] and 49% of over 65s say that their closest companions are the television or their pets.[3] In the USA, only 6% of

Americans over 60 say that they discuss important matters with anyone under 35 they are not related to.[4] Young and old are spending very little time together. People Like Me syndrome, as discussed in Chapter 6, is alive and well.

Is this okay? Is it just natural for us to be friends with people our own age?

Or are there unsung benefits to growing deep intergenerational connections? Are the divisions that exist between generations causing great harm to our society and could friendship be the answer?

Generations in the Bible

As a young Bible reader, I found myself bored and confused by the long historical lists of names of fathers and sons. I did not care about, nor see the relevance of, Zerubbabel the son of Shealtiel. And yet to the original authors, clearly these generational connections were of critical importance. The Jesus story must be passed from generation to generation. The psalmists continually urge us to make God's greatness known to our children and our children's children: 'We will not hide them from their descendants; we will tell the next generation the praiseworthy deeds of the LORD, his power, and the wonders he has done' (Psalm 78:4). Old and New Testaments model for us the power of successful succession: from Elijah to Elisha, Paul to Timothy, Jesus to the disciples. We will look at how we pass on the baton of faith, but for now let us consider how we receive it.

To help us do this, we are going to spend some time with Moses at a pivotal moment on his journey. His life has already been one of monumental drama and impact, having almost been killed as a baby, adopted into the Egyptian royal family, then called into defiance of the empire he has served. He has engaged in an epic plague-inducing power struggle with Pharaoh, centre stage at the defining moment of the Jewish exodus story, wielded his staff to part the Red Sea and lead a million people to liberation, overseen military conquest and negotiated miraculous provision of food and drink for his people with the living God. It's been eventful. And then comes a visit from his in-laws.

Jethro is the father of Moses' wife, Zipporah. We observe his important encounter with Moses in Exodus 18. Jethro brings both encouragement (verses 9–12) and critique (verses 17–23). At a time when he desperately needs it, the intervention of his father-in-law dramatically changes Moses' leadership style and releases him to have greater impact and well-being in the years ahead.

We all need Jethros in our lives. We need older, more spiritually mature, wiser and loving friends who have trodden the path ahead of us to help us find our way.

How do they help us? And how do we find them?

Proud parents

On Monday nights I take my son Caleb to football. I watch on as a pitch of 9-year-olds chase frantically after the ball, with enthusiasm far exceeding ability at this stage in their sporting development. When Caleb scores, once he has pulled off the trademark celebration of his latest footballing hero, he will look across at me for a moment of affirmation as if to say, 'Did you see that, Dad?' As I meet his eye with a smile and a punch of the air, I am reminded of the moments in my life when, in the highs of life, I have craved and received the encouragement that can only come from someone further down the road.

As a child there were many moments when I felt the warmth of parental praise. Since the death of my dad, it is one of the things I miss the most. His pride in me cannot quite be replaced, but I am grateful to have older, father-like figures in my life who have profoundly encouraged me at important times.

I was in my early 20s. I had just finished leading an exhausting week of ministry with teenagers, into which I had poured my heart and soul. I was ready for some pizza and a long night's sleep. I remember exactly where I was standing when a leadership team member, my friend Paul, bearhugged me and said, 'You've done great this week. I am proud of you.' The significance of that moment and its impact on my life was so great I will never forget it.

That's what Jethros do.

Moses is a man who struggles with his identity. He grows up without the stable influence of his birth parents. When he kills an Egyptian for beating a Hebrew, you sense the inner tension of a man who has grown up in one culture but knows where he is from. A third cultural identity is adopted when he flees to Midian and marries into it. No wonder he is the first person in the Bible to ask, 'Who am I?' (Exodus 3:11).

We need Jethros to remind us of our story, ground us in an identity bigger than ourselves and encourage us with their pride in what God is doing in our lives.

When Jethro shows up to meet Moses in the wilderness and hears what has happened, he is delighted and praises God, then eats with his son-in-law (Exodus 18:9–12). This is a deeply affirming act. There is something wonderful about knowing someone believes in you, has your back, wants what is best for you and can help you get there. Psychologist Steve Biddulph has found that if young boys have one good adult friend outside the family it significantly reduces the likelihood of juvenile crime.[5] Leonard Sweet puts it like this:

> Jethros bless you to go to what God is calling you to do so that you can receive peace in your life. Everyone needs someone (often older) who is wild and crazy about them, who believes in them, and cares enough about them to wake and shake them up to dream big and live large.[6]

Find friends further down the road of life and invite them to draw you forward, call out the gold in you and remind you of your identity and story.

All aboard the life coach

The Jethro story doesn't end there for Moses. His father-in-law does not simply tell him what a great job he is doing and move on. Moses allows Jethro to watch him as he spends a day being judge of the people as they bring their cases before him. It is rarely comfortable to allow people access to our lives, but the best of friends can be invited in to ask the difficult questions. And that is what Jethro does.

Mentors, take note. Jethro does not launch in with advice. Not yet. He first asks, 'What is this you are doing for the people? Why do you alone sit as judge, while all these people stand around you from morning to evening?' (Exodus 18:14). He listens to his son-in-law's response before telling him, 'What you are doing is not good' (verse 17). He then teaches him the art of delegation, and Moses puts the advice into practice.

I have a few mentor figures in my life. Some are permanent fixtures; others have been with me for temporary seasons. They are an invaluable source of advice, encouragement and critique. It is important to note that not every older friend is a mentor; intergenerational friendship in its own right is of immense worth. But I have found the passing on of wisdom that can only come with the benefit of experience is a key component of friendships with those older than me. When I speak to young adults, I often find they don't want a mentoring relationship; what they want is a genuine friendship with those older than them. But then what happens is that, in the context of this relationship, wisdom inescapably leaks between young and old.

The final observation of this relationship is that Jethro speaks to Moses from outside of the existing structures in Moses' life. Jethro is a Midianite, not a Hebrew. This gives him a helpful degree of neutrality when speaking into his son-in-law's situation. One challenge I have occasionally encountered is finding a voice with as little bias as possible. Mentors in your local church are unlikely to advise you to move away (unless they secretly despise you!). The same is probably true at work, if your boss cares about keeping you. At junction moments in my life, when making big changes, I have found golden counsel in trusted sages whose only agenda is God's will for my life. These are the best of older friends.

Finding a Jethro

Like many of those described in this book, friendships like this rarely just happen. We must be intentional about them.

Especially for the temporary mentoring relationships, timing is key. In Moses' life Jethro arrives for a few days and then Moses sends him 'on his way' (Exodus 18:27). (Not sure many of us would get away with that with our in-laws!) Many people's experiences of mentor figures is that they journey with them to support them at formative or pivotal moments in their lives.

The worlds of film, sport and reality TV are replete with examples of young heroes who need counsel and investment at a key moment on their quest. Yoda and Skywalker, Morpheus and Neo, Gandalf and Baggins, Dumbledore and Potter, Sir Alex and Ronaldo, X-Factor judges and wannabes. At a time in my life when I was asking big questions about my calling and destiny, I felt unable to journey and make big decisions alone. My inner circles were helpful, but I sensed God encourage me to seek wisdom from an older connection who was detached from my church and work life. I prayed about it and felt led to reach out to a family friend called Tom, who had been my dad's best mate. I asked him if we could meet once every couple of months to chat about life and the future. Those cups of coffee and walks round the park were priceless in helping me navigate a season of significant change.

There are other intergenerational friendships that last a lifetime. The church family can often be the best place to find these. Churches are one of the few places in our society where the generations gather so beautifully together. When I was at university, the only time I saw babies and pensioners was when I went to church. My sons are growing up with no living grandfathers, but our church is full of older generations of caring, godly men and women who are already taking the time to get to know them and filling some of the gap left by grandpas who died sooner than we would have liked.

A key question to ask when looking for a Jethro is this: who do I want to be like?

The rabbinic tradition was that disciples would choose a rabbi whose example they wanted to follow. The idea was not that they would learn in order to know what the teacher knew, but that they would become like them. It was about character rather than gifting. Finding a friend who is older than you and can bring the blessing of a Jethro can be as simple as asking who in your church family you admire and want to be like and then finding ways to spend time with them. More often than not, the benefit of these friendships turns out to be mutual.

Intergenerational relationships also have a profound effect on the quality of our discipleship. In *Faith for Exiles*, researchers David Kinnaman and Mark Matlock analyse research that explores the features of young adults who are thriving in their faith. They find that the presence of a 'faith champion' plays such an important role in making resilient young disciples that it cannot be overstated. 'Each young disciple needs champions outside their immediate family who follow Jesus and can sponsor their spiritual development – other adults who can shape them, speak into their lives, and help develop their gifts.'[7]

But they also require effort on our part. Kinnaman and Matlock observe: 'these kinds of relationship don't usually happen by accident. They require intentional planning and consistent effort from everyone involved.'[8] In most cases it is the younger of the parties who does this instigating. My view is that the onus lies with the Moses rather than the Jethro to reach out and suggest a meal or a coffee to get the ball rolling.

Take a moment to reflect on those who have played an important part in your life journey and thank God for them. We all stand on the shoulders of giants.

Shoulders

To the shoulders broad we have clambered upon,
The voices raw that have cheered us on,
To the hardened hands that have battled and fought,
This is a tribute to those who have taught us,
Encouraged us, willed us to thrive,
Who've handed us the wheel when they've wanted to drive.

To those who have listened to us when life has been poo,
To those we've looked at and said 'I want to be like you',
To the pastors and dream casters,
intercessors and ancestors,
game raisers and trail blazers,
old agers and back stagers,
up lifters and little gifters.

For the quiet words and the 'little chats'
That would keep us from a backslide,
And the many other times we've needed a kick up the backside.
For the cups of tea, the looks in the eyes,
For the cheers, the beers, the tears, the years of
Prayer and care and battle cries.

Take a two-pound coin and read around the rim.
For its inscriptions, indentations sing a deeper hymn,
Of the power of empowerment, the logic of alliance.
We stand on the shoulders of giants

And now to those trailing in our wake,
May their impact cause hell's deepest caverns to shake.
May others glide us in their slipstream in their time,
And may our shoulders be broad enough for others to climb.

All of us are influenced by the shoulders we stand on. For some of us the foundation is more stable than others, but all of us write our chapter between the pages of those who have gone before and those who follow our contribution. In the biblical genealogies, each name has those above and beneath it. With our lives and relationships, we build a platform for the next generation to build on. May our shoulders be broad enough for others to climb.

The apprentice

Success is found in succession.

At around the same time as Jethro's visit, the book of Exodus introduces us to Joshua. In the first significant battle after crossing the Red Sea, it is Joshua who selects and leads the army as Moses watches on. But it is after Jethro's visit that Joshua begins to be referred to as Moses' assistant (Exodus 24:13; 33:11; Numbers 11:28). Perhaps Jethro's investment in Moses encourages him to intensify his relationship with Joshua, or maybe Moses just instinctively knows that he will need to raise up a leader to pass the baton on to.

Just as we need those further down the track to call us forward, we get to play our part with the ones trailing behind us in the slipstream of life. There are few things more rewarding than seeing those we have invested in thrive and flourish. For thirteen years I worked for Youth for Christ and helped lead the youth ministry at our church. Moments of seeing young people stepping out of their comfort zones, empowered to lead, speak and serve, are imprinted indelibly on my memory.

One summer we had been away as a youth group to a Christian festival and several of the teenage lads had been captivated by the gospel and returned home desperate to keep the fiery passion alive and live for Jesus. With a friend, I made sure each of them had a Bible and commissioned them to read a chapter a day and highlight the verses that spoke to them. We arranged to meet at our house each week to discuss what they'd read and pray. The deal was that if you hadn't done your 'homework' you were not rewarded with time playing FIFA on the games console! When it started we had no idea the group would meet weekly until the boys became men. After a few years they had all read most of the New Testament and bonded in a profound way. Today most of that group are wholehearted followers of Jesus and I have no doubt that those Thursday afternoons were formative in the disciple-making process. My friend and I have done very little, but we lit a fire, and moreover we have good friendships with each of those lads and have journeyed with them into adulthood.

Charles Spurgeon said, 'Carve your name not on marble, but on hearts.' Our legacy lingers in our relationships. Never underestimate the power of investing in a Joshua.

Protégé pathways

What does this type of friendship look like? How do we learn together?

Moses' relationship with Joshua is instructive. First, he takes Joshua with him on significant journeys. There are few things better for any relationship than time spent going somewhere together. 'Then Moses set out with Joshua his assistant, and Moses went up on the mountain of God' (Exodus 24:13). As the older party, this can be a natural, relational way to get things started. I have regularly said to those I have been investing in, 'Do you want to come with me to this meeting? It would be fun to hang out.'

The power of journeying together can be found in the life of the famous missionary James Hudson Taylor. He instigated a work in China that led to the foundation of 125 schools, 18,000 Christian conversions and the empowerment of hundreds of workers. It didn't start well for him though. He had been in China for less than two years when he faced criticism from the established missionaries, isolation from his sending organization and local rejection from the British consul. On top of this his girlfriend wrote him a letter to let him know that she wasn't sure whether she loved him any more. It could have been the end of his ministry. He poured out his pain to his mother, 'My heart is sad, sad. I do not know what to do.' Enter William Burns, a fellow missionary from Scotland. He was about twenty years older than Hudson Taylor, and he took him under his wing. They simply travelled together for seven months, preaching and praying along the way. J. C. Pollock writes of this friendship, 'Burns saved Taylor from himself.'[9]

Key to these relationships especially is asking good questions and listening well. I am often asking my mentors, 'Why did you do that? How did you become good at that?' Leonard Sweet observes in his analysis of Paul and Timothy's mentoring relationship: 'if there were one word that indicates the success or failure of being Timothy, it would be this one: listening'.[10]

Second, Moses releases Joshua to have a go. It is Joshua who is sent in the search party into Canaan in Numbers 13, and when Moses is nearing death, his protégé is appointed as his successor (Numbers 27:18). Releasing and empowering is a dangerous business. Our apprentices will do either a better or a worse job than us. If they do better than us, it is easy to get insecure. If they do worse, our judgement can be questioned. At some point we step back and let them fly.

When my mum died, I had the moving privilege of being with her for her final moments. During the preceding days she had asked to hear songs and have the Bible read to her. One of the songs I sang over her was 'The Blessing'. The lyrics speak of the favour of God over a thousand generations, children of children. I pictured the baton of faith passing from my mum, a giant of Christian faith and example to me, to my sons and then on to their unborn children and beyond. We stand on the shoulders of giants and spend our lives broadening our shoulders so that future generations may stand tall on the legacy we build.

The tragedy in the Jethro–Moses–Joshua story comes at the beginning of the book of Judges. There are some harrowing words. 'After that whole generation had been gathered to their ancestors, another generation grew up who knew neither the LORD nor what he had done for Israel' (Judges 2:10). It seems that Joshua was an outstanding mentee, but a woeful mentor. May we be both inspired by the benefits of intergenerational relationship and take sober warning from the consequences of not investing in the future.

In this chapter we have added another couple of circles of friends. I realize one of the questions you may have is: how do I make time for more types of connection without being overwhelmed? I hope as we have journeyed through the levels of friendship you have been released from the guilt of having to be good friends with everyone. It is likely that these intergenerational friendships will appear in your network layer rather than your huddle or inner circle. Getting together does not need to be as frequent as in your closer layers. There may also be more regular contact for a short period of time, as was the case with my friend Tom. The important thing is that they are present in some form. We need Jethros and Joshuas.

The best of amends: top friendship tips

Say thank you

I hope, as we have reflected on those who form us, God has brought to mind key players in your journey. Whose shoulders do you stand on? Whose are the voices that have spoken life, correction and encouragement to you? Many of them will not know the impact they have had. Stop reading for a moment and write a list of those who have parented, pastored and prioritized you. Consider how you might thank them. Write a letter, make a call, buy them a coffee, send them a copy of this book! Don't leave them wondering about the impact they have had; it may well inspire them to keep investing in others.

Age audit

Reach for the circles you drew at the end of the last chapter. As you cast your eyes over the names again, make a mental note of those who are a different age from you. It is likely most will be a similar age to you, but there may be some who stand out as particularly older or younger. Consider whether they might be a Jethro or a Joshua to you. Who are those in your circles whose character you look at and aspire to emulate? Who could you invest in to help them forward on their journey? If there are obvious gaps here, this may be an area to pray into and ask God to provide spiritual parents and protégés for you.

I'm pleased to let you know we have saved the best until last. Our circles so far have covered friendship close and distant, similar and diverse, lifelong and fleeting, old and young. It's time to talk about the one circle that surrounds them all. Let me introduce you to the best of friends.

The themes of this chapter can be explored further using small-group resources, videos and discussion questions. Delve deeper at: www.philknox.co.uk

Further reading

N. Allen and M. Allen, *The XYZ of Discipleship* (Malcolm Down Publishing, 2020). Nick and Marjorie lead a thriving church of young adults. This is a helpful overview of the lessons they have learned and the values they lead with.

D. Kinnaman and M. Matlock, *Faith for Exiles* (Baker Books, Grand Rapids MI, 2019). After explaining the factors behind why young adults are leaving the church in *You Lost Me*, Kinnaman and Matlock explore the characteristics of resilient young disciples.

R. Perrin, *Changing Shape* (SCM Press, London, 2020). Ruth is a leading voice in young adult ministry in the UK. This is the culmination of her research into how we disciple this generation fruitfully.

10

+ (add) – Moses had a God

God is more of a friend than a formula.
(John Mark Comer, *God Has a Name*)

On 7 June 2015 the *Daily Mail* reported that Jesus had been spotted in IKEA. Shoppers were stopped dead in their tracks as they noticed the face of Christ staring at them from the pattern in the wood of the door to the gentleman's toilet in the Braehead branch. 'I went to the toilet and I met God,' stated a startled father of three. Another customer lamented, 'I actually went for tie-backs for curtains, but they didn't have any. So Jesus didn't help us there.'

How we view God really matters. Author and theologian A. W. Tozer stated: 'What comes to our mind when we think about God is the most important thing about us.'[1] And it is not surprising that when it comes to relating to the all-powerful creator of the universe, the Bible offers us a range of facets and features to the relationship, which we read about as different titles, names and roles. He is our Father, Saviour, Judge, King, Provider, Sustainer, Example and Teacher.

But don't miss this. God is also our Friend.

And his friendship is more important than any human connection.

Feel far from God? This bit is for you

If you are reading this and you are not yet a Christian, these are the most important paragraphs you will read in this book. I hope you have celebrated with me the beauty and power of relationship as you have got this far. I wonder if, in doing so, it has caused you to consider whether that connection you have felt to someone else might be an echo of an even more powerful friendship that could be possible. I want you to know, in no uncertain terms, that the best news in the universe is that a friendship with God is not only possible, it is freely available.

It doesn't matter who you are, what you have done, where you are from, how broken, religious, messed up or perfect you are; you can know and be known by the author of your story and the inventor of friendship. And his deepest desire is to know you and welcome you home.

God's hand of friendship is outstretched to you. Will you take it?

If you tracked the story of your relationship with God, whatever your starting point is, he is 'all in'. Do not be in any doubt: you are loved – firmly, unswervingly, unconditionally, fiercely and relentlessly.

But in friendship terms, we all know we have not been the best of friends to God. The same old enemies of distraction, our selfishness and self-centredness drive wedges between us and we feel, almost tangibly, a distance between us and our maker. We experience a dim reflection of this ultimate relationship in our friendships, marriages and families, but they fall short of completing us. There is a painful disconnect between us. Like star-crossed lovers, distant relations or long-lost friends, the gap seems irreconcilable. But God does not give up. 'Greater love has no one than this: to lay down one's life for one's friends' (John 15:13).

The life, death and resurrection of Jesus Christ is the definitive point in history. It is also game-changing for friendship. He exemplifies what it looks like for us and enables it to happen with God.

As his arms are outstretched in self-sacrifice on a cruel wooden cross, Jesus is the epitome of true friendship. As his soul cries, 'It is finished,' Jesus absorbs the power of our sin and selfishness, meaning that reconciliation and relationship are possible with the king of the universe. And when crucifixion cannot contain him, when death defeated dare not destroy him, his resurrection invites us to a new life, free from our frailties and failings, with relationships reborn.

Friendship with God is not just for religious people; it is for everyone. And it really matters. Just as the quality and quantity of your physical life is increased by how good your relationships are, if you want the best possible life now and the absolute assurance of a life beyond the grave, a relationship with God is not just a nice addition for some, but the one connection that you need above all others.

Your acceptance of his friendship offer is the single most important decision you could ever make. It is forgiveness for your past, his presence in your present and hope for the future.

Don't miss it. With all that I am I want to urge you to make friends with the one who made you and become who you were created to be. I'm praying for you as you read on and if this is your moment, there's a simple prayer you can pray at the end of this chapter to choose to embrace God's offer to you.

In its right place

If you are already a follower of Jesus, I hope that you have not only rejoiced with me in just how good friendship is, but have observed, while reading this book, the impact that knowing Jesus has on your relationships. Christians really should be the best of friends to all those around them; we have the architect of relationship living within us, and the life we are called to, of love, generosity and self-sacrifice, in the example of Jesus, should make for spectacular friend-making material. Moreover, the hallmark by which Jesus said we would be recognized as his followers was not our religious practices, cheesy Christian T-shirts or fishy car stickers, but by the quality of our relationships: 'By this everyone will know that you are my disciples, if you love one another' (John 13:35).

Our defining characteristic and most recognizable feature as Christians is the way we love one another.

What if that were true? What if that were what they said about us? Friendship really is a masterpiece of the greatest artist of them all.

But sometimes good things can become elevated above their pay grade or, in worship terms, their praise-grade.

Friendolatry

I love sport. I am captivated by the passion, the story, the breathtaking moments of genius and its power to unite and divide. Sport is a good thing, a God-given thing. But sometimes our love for the created can exceed our love for the creator. And I have, at times, allowed my sporting fervour to surpass my devotion to my saviour. In late 2014, I felt so convicted and challenged by how important it had become that I decided to fast from watching, playing and thinking and talking about all sport for a year. So 2015 was a barren desert of sport-less activity. Amusingly, when I called the TV provider to cancel my sports package and they asked me why I was abandoning the service, they had to add a new category of 'Religious Fast'. My wife describes it as one of the best years of her life. New Year's Day 2016 was one of my greatest days ever.

In the same way, friendship is one of God's best ideas, but it must be kept in its rightful place. The only way to do this is to let all of your friendship circles be encircled by the great Connector. Dallas Willard, using similar imagery, is worth quoting here:

Ultimately every human circle is doomed to dissolution if it is not caught up in the life of the only genuinely self-sufficient circle of sufficiency, that of the Father, Son, and Holy Spirit.

For that circle is the only one that is truly and totally self-sufficient. And all the broken circles must ultimately find their healing there, if anywhere.[2]

All friends will let us down at some point. That's why we need the one circle of friends that will not fail us. Because relational connection is so beneficial it is easy to see how it can become idolatry; indeed, some conclude of our culture that God has been replaced with a new holy trinity of friends, family and self.[3] Friends provide much-needed advice, approval and affection, but when we go to them for these things first, before we primarily get our identity, insight and intimacy from the Father, this is a warning sign that our friendships have climbed on to the throne of our hearts.

The order in which Jesus' greatest commandments are placed matters. We love God first and our friends second. When we do, both relationships are strengthened. You cannot be the best of friends without God at the centre of your life. Only when you experience the expansive love of God can it fill you to the measure where it flows out into all your relationships to its fullest extent. The first step to building stronger connections with others is building a stronger connection with God.

FaceTime

What might this stronger connection look like?

To answer this question, let's circle back to the prominent characters and themes of this book.

As we examined the power of and pressure on friendship, two foundational friendship features were time and presence. Jesus often retreated to lonely places and prayed; his relationship with the Father surpassed any of his earthly connections. Then there was Moses. What was his relationship with God like?

'The LORD would speak to Moses face to face, as one speaks to a friend' (Exodus 33:11). When you read the account of his extraordinary life, from burning bush to Red Sea, from Sinai to Nebo, a consistent theme is the presence of God in his life, something he relentlessly pursued. And through this pursuit came the right to talk to God face to face.

Moses was the original FaceTimer.

Time.

Presence.

These are intrinsic ingredients to a friendship with God.

But where Moses' experience of intimate relationship with his creator was the exception rather than the rule in the Old Testament, the life, death and resurrection of Jesus has meant that all of us can know God's presence with us in a real and active way if we choose to spend time with him. In 2 Corinthians 3, Paul describes how, after spending time with God, Moses' face would shine with the glory he had encountered, but also how he would cover his face so that his people would not see the glow diminishing. His encouragement is that, through the Spirit of God, face coverings are no longer needed, because the presence of God is here to stay in our hearts and lives (verses 7–18).

Let's dwell on this for a moment. It can be easy to have a mindset that reflects Moses' experience of friendship with God rather than what is possible now. How often do we talk about our church services as 'going into the presence of God', as if he is absent during the rest of the week? Do we talk and act as though our Sundays are when we have FaceTime with God and then allow the glory to fade from Monday to Saturday? Do we treat our relationship with the great Connector as if he is in one of our outer friendship circles?

It was a cold October day. Andy and I set off early in the morning to be there for the very moment the theme park opened. Strategically we had chosen a day in the low season, when the attraction would be quiet due to most children and teenagers being at school. My roller-coaster-enthusiast friend and I rushed around the rides with abandon. The digital displays that inform you how many hours' wait you will face in the queues were redundant. On some amusements there were so few people they just kept going round. It was bliss.

By lunchtime we had conquered the majority of the most popular thrills and our adrenaline levels were peaking. We sat down for some much-needed sustenance to fuel us for the afternoon and sat on a bench at the entrance to the log-flume ride, eating overpriced chicken burgers. We watched mostly empty log carriages emerging from a small tunnel at the top of a hill, then hurtling down the hill and being enveloped in the splash at the bottom. Due to the chilly temperature it was not a popular day for log-fluming. Until a young boy arrived with his dad.

He was probably about 10 years old. He probably should have been in school. But when he saw a log hit the water and the resultant ten-foot wave, he was captivated. His face lit up as if it were Christmas morning. His dad, however, not enthused by the prospect of a soaking on a bitter autumn afternoon, was not keen. The pleading and begging began, but the father was not budging. Eventually, a compromise was reached and the son was allowed to go on the ride alone while his dad watched him and held the bags.

No more than five minutes later another dad arrived on the scene. With him were three teenage girls. At the same sight of a damp roller coaster, his joy was uncontainable and dwarfed even the previous boy's excitement. He immediately grabbed the hands of his family members without giving them time to object, and flew towards the ride. 'Come on, girls! We're going on the log flume!'

God is like the second dad.

It is easy to feel that his presence with us is limited to religious moments and that when the time comes for us to go about our daily lives, he lets us go on our own and holds the bags. The truth is found in the most common promise in the Bible: 'I will be with you.'

But like the simplest offer of friendship, invitation to spend time together or request to connect on social media, we must accept the offer of his presence. God is not like a friend forcing himself into our life; the promise of his company is always there waiting to be acknowledged. So how might we even begin to relate daily, hourly, to the creator of the cosmos? Let's return to Jesus' example.

Purposeful plans and relentless receptivity

Jesus demonstrated both intentional time carved out to be with his Father and an openness to appreciate his presence with him and respond to his leading. It is challenging to read that even when Jesus was most in demand, at a time of prolific and pressing ministry, he got up early, left the house and went to be alone so that he could pray (Mark 1:35). Those closest to him seem surprised at this emphasis in priorities and told him, 'Everyone is looking for you' (Mark 1:37). I know that when my life gets busy, when the demands for my time exceed my capacity, a convenient casualty can be the time I spend with God. Mark seems to be deliberate in showing us that as Jesus got busier, he got more purposeful about carving out time to pray.

These rhythms were a consistent part of the Son of God's life. We are told that Jesus went out 'as usual' to the Mount of Olives (Luke 22:39), and yet we also see that alongside these regular times acknowledging the presence of his Father, he was constantly aware of and alert to him too. He only did what he saw his Father doing (John 5:19) and used the imagery of being attached to a vine as a picture of connectivity and dependence (John 15:1–8). In digital terms there are deliberate moments of checking in online, but the Wi-Fi is also always on, recognizing the presence of God and being open to his leading and prompting throughout our waking moments.

What does this mean for us? In maintaining a thriving friendship with God, we need intentional rhythms that prioritize time with him, listening to him through reading the Bible and times of silence in a noise-polluted world. We also need an 'always on' mentality to appreciating God's presence with us on the mountaintops and plains, and in the valleys of life, in a culture where we have never been more entertained or distracted. In the waking gratitude of a new day, as the warmth of sunlight hits our face, in the embrace of a loved one, before the stress of a difficult meeting at work, in the heart-sinking moment as a bad-news text message illuminates our phone, in the laughter of coffee with mates, in the regret of a silly decision, in the breath-taking beauty of a sunset, in the calm and exhaustion as our head hits the pillow, and a million more scenarios, the art of friendship with God is recognizing, celebrating, inviting and pursuing his presence before us, around us, beside us and within us in the extreme and the extra-ordinary, the mundane and the monotonous.

God is your friend. Don't miss the scandalous beauty of this truth or take for granted the generous invitation to spend time in his presence.

The best of amends: top friendship tips

Here are three practical ways to invest in your friendship with God.

God's presence in our habits

Don't give God your dregs. We are creatures of habit. Even the most disorganized among us can form meaningful and healthy routines to help us function as human beings. Few of us forget to brush our teeth before bed. Find and prioritize a regular moment each day to stop, pray, read your Bible, talk to God, listen and invest in the most important friendship you have. For me, that looks like a cup of tea as soon as I wake up, sitting at the kitchen table with my dog-eared Bible, a colourful journal, the same pen and a variety of accompanying prayer and reading guides. Sometimes I go for a walk. I don't always get it right, but I want to give my best friend my best time.

God's presence in nature

The Bible reminds us that the heavens declare God's glory (Psalm 19:1). It is a constant source of amusement to my family that when a scenic view emerges while on holiday, I emit an effervescent 'WOW!' that startles the car into laughter and eye-rolling. I'm frequently captivated by an exquisite sunset, a towering mountain, a shimmering sea or a night sky replete with dazzling gem-like stars. I am overcome with wide-eyed wonder when staring at an idyllic vista dripping with natural beauty. And in these moments, I experience the intimacy and closeness of a God whose fingerprints cover the scene that surrounds me. When you next find yourself in a similar environment, take a moment to appreciate his majesty, magnitude and affection for you.

God's presence when together

Jesus said: 'where two or three gather in my name, there am I with them' (Matthew 18:20). In a book about relationship, here is an inevitable yet necessary encouragement to be part of a church and prioritize gathering to meet with each other and God. Make every effort not to miss the moments when your church family come together. Your presence matters to them, and their connection with you is a lifeline to spiritual health. But it is also an important means by which we encounter God as we worship together, learn together and interact with one another.

A prayer to accept God's offer of friendship

If you found you were interested in accepting God's offer of friendship as you read the section above, 'Feel far from God? This bit is for you', take time to pray this prayer. With these simple words you communicate to God that you want to turn away from trusting in yourself and make him the most important thing in your life.

God, I am sorry where I have got stuff wrong.
I want to turn my life around.

Thank you that you died and rose again for me.
I want to follow you and accept your offer of friendship.
Amen.

These are not magic words, but deciding to pray them and mean them is the most important decision you will ever make. Jesus said that when one sinner repents, the angels throw a party (Luke 15:10). If you have connected with God in this way, let another Christian know and go to <www.philknox.co.uk> to find some resources to help you on the next steps of your journey.

Further reading

M. Greenwood, *The Journey: Taking your next steps* (Verite, Worthing, 2021). If you prayed the prayer to accept God's offer of friendship, here is your next move. Mark has been helping people take their first steps for decades and this is a brilliant start to a journey of faith.

P. Greig, *How to Pray* (Hodder & Stoughton, London, 2019). This is a prayer guide for a new or seasoned Christian, in which Pete journeys through the Lord's Prayer and inspires us to spend more time with Jesus.

J. John, *Making the Connection* (Philo Trust, Rickmansworth, 2015). A concise and memorable expansion on my explanation of connecting with God, which includes valuable advice on taking friendship with God to the next level.

D. Ortlund, *Deeper* (Crossway, Wheaton IL, 2021). This is a simple, beautifully crafted book that asks how we grow as Christians and expertly balances our responsibility and God's in the process.

Conclusion

After a twenty-four-hour shift as a firefighter, Matt Swatzell was driving home when, overcome with exhaustion, he momentarily fell asleep at the wheel. As a result his car drifted across the central reservation and he hit an oncoming car. In that car was June Fitzgerald and her 1-year-old daughter, Faith. June was also seven months pregnant.

Matt remembers the moment when the police officer walked into his hospital room to inform him that June and her unborn baby had been killed in the accident.

In the same hospital, June's husband Erik was receiving the news that would change his life for ever. His present was agony, his future uncertain.

Erik was then asked by prosecutors about pressing charges of wrongdoing on the man who had killed his wife and child. In that moment he decided to choose grace and mercy, and encouraged the judge to pursue a lenient sentence of a fine and community service.

Two years passed from that October day in 2006, then Erik and Matt met coincidentally outside a grocery store and Erik began to walk towards the man who had changed his life. Matt was over-whelmed by the emotion of the moment and started to weep uncontrollably. Erik just embraced him and reassured him of his forgiveness. Matt describes that hug as the biggest relief of his life. The two of them spent the next couple of hours talking and getting to know one another.

But that was not the end. Both men felt a connection to the other, as though they were meant to be friends, and their relationship is now over a decade strong. Matt describes Erik as a big brother, and the families regularly spend time together. Erik is a pastor and both he and Matt see God's hand in connecting them.[1]

Forgiveness. Honesty. Grace. Vulnerability. Intentionality. A relationship forged, in part, by the great Connector. These are features of the best of friends.

And the reminder that friendship, far from being a fairy tale, is the costly everyday involvement and investment in real, messy lives.

The story of Erik and Matt's connection is also a powerful display of how great friends emerge from the ashes of brokenness and despair.

It's a tale of resurrection.

At these extraordinary times in our world, we desperately need deeper bonds of trust between each other. Healing for the nations is found in relationship; it's not what you know, it's who you know. I hope, wherever you are on your journey of faith, that reading this book has drawn you closer to the best of friends, the one who sticks closer than a brother. And I pray that you have a fresh appreciation of how our connections can change the small piece of the world we are given, but also the very fabric of our society.

Life is relentless. I feel daily the pressures of work, church and 'life admin'. I wake up each day determined to be the best husband and dad I can be. For my own well-being I need moments in solitude and time spent exercising my aging body. In all these components of life I am doing my best to follow Jesus and bring hope to the world around me. I often feel I am at war with the clock and the time slots in my diary. And in this war, my friendships are so often the casualties on the frontline.

They are worth fighting for.

When relationships are drifting and months have passed since that failed attempt to meet up for coffee, when we reach for an excuse to avoid accepting an important invitation to connect with people different from us, when a close friend reaches out at an inconvenient time, we must remember how important our relationships are to the fabric of our being. Intentionality matters. The fight for friendship matters.

When life is less than perfect, when squalls rock the boat, when we do something we are ashamed of, when we crave the comfort of self-pity and seclusion, we must battle the tendency to retreat into ourselves and become isolated. Vulnerability matters. The fight for friendship matters.

And when we have been hurt, when the sting of betrayal lingers and its poison bides and binds, when the desire to build a fortress of protection feels greater than the risk of letting the soul's defended barricades down, we must, with wisdom, go again and make room in our wounded hearts for others. Forgiveness matters. The fight for friendship matters.

There is a cost to friendship.

Looking after ourselves is important. There is a truth at the heart of the great commandment to love our neighbour *as ourselves*; to give the best of ourselves we need to love ourselves well. But in a world where self-help books monumentally outnumber books about helping others, the pendulum has swung towards therapeutic individualism over sacrificial friendship. As individuals, as a society, as a church and as friends, we must redress the balance.

May our casualties be the effort we make to drive across town to catch up, the indulgence we forgo to bless a friend in financial need, the hour's sleep we sacrifice listening to the mate who just needs to talk. We must fight the egocentric and external narratives that exhort us to always look after number one. There is no greater love than those who lay down their lives for their friends.

As I have written this book, I have frequently stopped and closed my eyes in deep appreciation of the friends who bless my life. I hope there have been similar moments, as you have read, of gratitude and indebtedness to your connections. I pray that these words have given you fresh passion to pursue depth beyond superficiality, vulnerability before triviality, quality over quantity.

May the words spoken at the dawn of time ring true in our lives: it is not good for men and women to be alone. May the world have fewer lonely people. May our relational circles look more like those of the great Connector. May we celebrate and cultivate one of God's greatest gifts to us. And may we experience the best of friends, be the best of friends and know the Best Friend of them all.

Afterword

It was one of those situations where I had requested a particular speaker for a particular event. The speaker was not available so someone else was recommended. And that's how I met Phil . . .

The event included a gathering of more than a hundred church leaders from many different denominations. In the midst of this, Phil turned up with his wife and two children. His task was to bring a gospel message on the main stage at Trafalgar Square – without knowing who'd be in the crowd. Phil, in his animated, effervescent way, presented a message that resonated in the hearts of everyone who heard his voice.

That was the beginning of our friendship.

Everything that was said about Phil when he was recommended was true. I was told that he was committed to real connections, relationships and friendships, and I have found this to be indeed so. Since our first meeting, our relationship has developed and it is not uncommon for us to meet and spend hours talking about life, the church, society and many other things. Phil is not merely a transactional person. Rather, in faithful obedience to Jesus' teaching, Phil prioritizes meaningful friendships and deep relationships.

Where there is deep friendship, there are also great possibilities for doing great things in our marriages, wider family networks, among work colleagues and within local churches. Deep friendships equate to enormous potential on many levels.

Every Sunday, millions of people around the world attend church and thousands more tune in over social media. However, there seems to be a real lack of true friendships fostered through these channels. Sure, we have a lot of 'fellowship' going on in various ways, but very little friendship.

Phil's book helps us to understand what friendship really is and then to pursue and value true friendship in a way that will be beneficial to the individuals who claim to be friends. It explores principles that can be applied to enrich all the relationships that we are engaged in as we journey through this life.

The book is invaluable because exercising true friendship is costly and requires us to be vulnerable and possibly to get hurt. Phil reminds us that we all need friends – people who will walk with us through life's ups and downs. He also challenges us to confront the notion that friendship is what is so commonly conducted these days through text messages or WhatsApp or whatever social media platform we may use. Rather, friendship is about creating the space and time to be in one another's company – to be present to laugh or cry, to listen in the silence, to eat and to talk.

This book is relevant, timely and a reminder that we are not made to live on an island by ourselves. We were made to be relational. We need friends.

Les Isaac OBE
President, Ascension Trust

Notes

Introduction

1 <www.thegospelcoalition.org/blogs/kevin-deyoung/the-gift-of-friendship-and-the-godliness-of-good-friends-part-1/>

1 The power of friendship

1 <www.bbc.co.uk/news/education-47043831>

2 <www.forbes.com/quotes/10361/>

3 J. Holmes, *The Company We Keep: In search of biblical friendship* (Cruciform Press, Minneapolis MN, 2014), p. 19.

4 Clearly an important application of this verse is the need for marriage – God creates a wife for Adam after all – but it also has wider application in terms of friends and community, and this is the emphasis I am making here.

5 For example, see <https://pubmed.ncbi.nlm.nih.gov/21895364/> and <www.sciencedaily.com/releases/2011/10/111026091229.htm>.

6 R. Dunbar, *Friends* (Little, Brown, London, 2021), p. 11.

7 <www.mentalhealth.org.uk/news/millions-still-feeling-hopeless-lockdown-eases-new-briefing-mental-health-foundation>

8 <www.theguardian.com/society/2019/feb/05/youth-unhappiness-uk-doubles-in-past-10-years>

9 D. Smith, *God's Plan for Your Wellbeing* (CWR, Farnham, Surrey, 2020), p. 123.

10 Dunbar, *Friends*, p. 20.

11 <https://source.wustl.edu/2010/03/meaningful-conversation-may-be-key-to-happiness/>

12 J. Wesley, *The Heart of John Wesley's Journal* (Hendrickson, Peabody MA, 2015), p. 11.

13 R. Huntley, *The World According to Y* (Allen & Unwin, Crows Nest NSW), p. 28.

14 <www.theatlantic.com/entertainment/archive/2017/02/each-day-is-galentines-day/516408/>

2 The pressure on friendship

1 <https://yougov.co.uk/topics/relationships/articles-reports/2019/09/25/quarter-britons-dont-have-best-friend>

2 <www.statista.com/statistics/1222815/loneliness-among-adults-by-country/>

3 J. M. Comer, *Live No Lies* (Form, London, 2021), p. xxiii.

4 <https://ourworldindata.org/working-hours>

5 <www.ons.gov.uk/employmentandlabourmarket/peopleinwork/employmentandemployeetypes/articles/familiesandthelabourmarketengland/2019>

6 <www.researchgate.net/publication/263518303_The_Knowledge_Economy_How_Knowledge_is_Reshaping_the_Economic_Life_of_Nations>

7 <https://blogs.gartner.com/craig-roth/2019/12/11/2019-exceeded-1-billion-knowledge-workers/>

8 <www.forbes.com/sites/forbestechcouncil/2020/12/10/the-year-of-the-knowledge-worker/?sh=7934ded57fbb>

9 K. DeYoung, *Crazy Busy* (Crossway, Wheaton IL, 2013), p. 26.

10 V. Roberts, *True Friendship* (10Publishing, Leyland, 2013), p. 30.

11 J. Yates, *Fractured* (HarperNorth, Manchester, 2021), p. 118.

12 Yates, *Fractured*, p. 119.

13 <www.studyfinds.org/survey-the-average-adult-will-watch-more-than-78000-hours-of-tv/>

14 <www.independent.co.uk/tech/netflix-downloads-sleep-biggest-competition-video-streaming-ceo-reed-hastings-amazon-prime-sky-go-now-tv-a7690561.html>

15 <www.ons.gov.uk/peoplepopulationandcommunity/
    leisureandtourism/articles/youngpeoplespend
    athirdoftheirleisuretimeondevices/2017-12-19>

16 S. Turkle, *Alone Together* (Basic Books, New York, 2011), p. 1.

17 Youth For Christ, 'Gen Z: Rethinking Culture' (2017) available
    through: <https://yfc.co.uk/rethinkingculture/>

18 <https://www.princes-trust.org.uk/about-the-trust/news-views/
    ebay-youth-index-2019>

19 J. Lynch, *The Scent of Lemons* (Darton, Longman and Todd,
    London, 2012), p. 53.

20 R. Dunbar, *Friends* (Little, Brown, London, 2021), p. 348.

21 <www.huffpost.com/entry/text-breakup-_n_4922063>

22 <www.paultripp.com/articles/posts/getting-to-the-heart-of-your-
    words>

23 Comer, *Live No Lies*, p. 99.

3 Circles of friends

1 C. S. Lewis, *The Four Loves* (William Collins, London, 2012),
   p. 78.

2 H. Black, *Friendship* (Fleming H. Revell, Chicago IL, 1903), p. 3.

3 W. K. Rawlins, *Friendship Matters* (Transaction Publishers, New
   Brunswick NJ, 1992), p. 17.

4 R. Dunbar, *Grooming, Gossip and the Evolution of Language*
   (Harvard University Press, Cambridge MA, 1996), p. 77.

5 R. Dunbar, *Friends* (Little, Brown, London, 2021), p. 25.

6 Dunbar, *Friends*, p. 25.

7 Tilborg in S. Summers, *Friendship: Exploring its implications for
   the Church in postmodernity* (T&T Clark, London, 2009), p. 26.

4 One – Jesus had a best friend

1 M. Gladwell, *The Tipping Point* (Little, Brown, London, 2000),
   p. 38.

2 Gladwell, *The Tipping Point*, p. 38.

3 J. Holmes, *The Company We Keep: In search of biblical friendship* (Cruciform Press, Minneapolis MN, 2014), p. 108.

4 C. S. Lewis, *The Four Loves* (William Collins, London, 2012), p. 78.

5 R. Dunbar, *Friends* (Little, Brown, London, 2021), p. 203.

6 Holmes, *The Company We Keep*, p. 108.

7 <https://journals.sagepub.com/doi/pdf/10.1177/0265407518761225>

8 A. Fernando, *Reclaiming Friendship* (IVP, Leicester, 1991), pp. 17–18.

9 A. A. Milne, *The House at Pooh Corner* (Methuen & Co., London, 1928).

10 <www.ncbi.nlm.nih.gov/pmc/articles/PMC6913704>

11 <www.pnas.org/content/112/45/13811>

12 J. R. R. Tolkien, *The Return of the King* (HarperCollins, London, 2020), p. 948.

13 <www.sciencedaily.com/releases/2018/02/180226122506.htm>

14 Fernando, *Reclaiming Friendship*, p. 23.

15 Holmes, *The Company We Keep*, p. 31.

16 <www.focusonthefamily.com/episodes/broadcast/sharing-wisdom-with-the-next-generation-part-2-of-2/>

17 J. Collins, *Good to Great* (Random House, London, 2001), p. 1.

18 Fernando, *Reclaiming Friendship*, p. 17.

19 L. Sweet, *11* (David C. Cook, Colorado Springs CO, 2008), p. 51.

20 P. Parker, *The Art of Gathering* (Penguin, London, 2018), p. 131.

21 M. Walker, *Why We Sleep* (Penguin, London, 2017).

5 Three – Jesus had an inner circle

1 C. S. Lewis, *The Four Loves* (William Collins, London, 2012), p. 74.

2 H. Lee, *To Kill a Mockingbird* (Arrow, London, 1960), p. 228.

3 Lewis, *The Four Loves*, p. 72.

4 W. Hill, *Spiritual Friendship: Finding love in the church as a celibate gay Christian* (Brazos Press, Grand Rapids MI, 2015), p. xii.

5 P. Parker, *The Art of Gathering* (Penguin, London, 2018), p. 51.

6 <www.ncbi.nlm.nih.gov/pmc/articles/PMC3273616/>

7 A. Sow and A. Friedman, *Big Friendship: How we keep each other close* (Simon & Schuster, New York, 2021), p. 97.

8 <https://forge.medium.com/stretching-is-the-key-to-long-lasting-friendships-a64cc9429778>

9 A. Fernando, *Reclaiming Friendship* (IVP, Leicester, 1991), p. 147.

10 <https://twitter.com/robertmadu/status/357294607324815361>

6 Twelve – Jesus had a huddle

1 P. Parker, *The Art of Gathering* (Penguin, London, 2018), p. 51.

2 See B. Schwartz, *The Paradox of Choice* (Harper Perennial, New York, 2004).

3 <www.theguardian.com/lifeandstyle/2015/oct/21/choice-stressing-us-out-dating-partners-monopolies>

4 Phil's editor, Tom, adds, 'History has also called him "confessing Thomas", believing based on evidence, and ultimately dying on mission.' Doubters can do great things.

5 J. MacArthur, *Twelve Ordinary Men* (Nelson Books, Nashville TN, 2002), p. 73.

6 MacArthur, *Twelve Ordinary Men*, pp. 179–180.

7 J. Yates, *Fractured* (HarperNorth, Manchester, 2021), pp. 20–22.

8 <https://yougov.co.uk/topics/politics/articles-reports/2018/05/03/one-third-white-britons-dont-have-any-friends-ethn>

9 <www.nytimes.com/2016/09/01/upshot/a-question-about-friends-reveals-a-lot-about-class-divides.html>

10 <https://cordis.europa.eu/article/id/174939-the-effect-of-socioeconomic-segregation-on-european-cities>

11 T. Keller, *The Meaning of Marriage* (Dutton, New York, 2011), p. 114.

12 R. Dunbar, *Friends* (Little, Brown, London, 2021), pp. 162–163.

7 Seventy-two – Jesus had a network

1 R. I. Wilberforce and S. Wilberforce, *The Life of William Wilberforce*, abridged edn (London, 1843), p. 48.

2 S. Tomkins, *William Wilberforce – A Biography* (Lion Hudson, Oxford, 2007), p. 57.

3 <http://nationalmarriageproject.org/wordpress/wp-content/uploads/2014/08/NMP-BeforeIDoReport-Final.pdf>

4 <https://snap.stanford.edu/class/cs224w-readings/granovetter73weakties.pdf>

5 See <https://talkingjesus.org/2015-research/>.

6 P. Knox, *Story Bearer: How to share your faith with your friends* (IVP, London, 2020).

7 S. Chan, *Evangelism in a Skeptical World* (Zondervan, Grand Rapids MI, 2018), p. 43.

8 Chan, *Evangelism in a Skeptical World*, p. 43.

9 R. Butterfield, *The Gospel Comes with a House Key* (Crossway, Wheaton IL, 2018), pp. 92–93.

10 <www.about.sainsburys.co.uk/news/latest-news/2021/12-01-21-new-research-reveals-family-dinnertime>

11 J. Holmes, *The Company We Keep: In search of biblical friendship* (Cruciform Press, Minneapolis MN, 2014), p. 67.

12 <www.theguardian.com/society/2018/may/23/the-friend-effect-why-the-secret-of-health-and-happiness-is-surprisingly-simple>

13 A. Fernando, *Reclaiming Friendship* (IVP, Leicester, 1991), p. 70.

14 <www.eauk.org/assets/files/downloads/Changing-church-autumn-survey-disicipleship-evangelism-and-community-engagement.pdf>

15 W. Hill, *Spiritual Friendship: Finding love in the church as a celibate gay Christian* (Brazos Press, Grand Rapids MI, 2015), p. 110.

16 A. Sow and A. Friedman, *Big Friendship: How we keep each other close* (Simon & Schuster, New York, 2021), p. 147.

8 Add a zero – Jesus had a following

1 B. Milne, *The Message of John* (IVP, Leicester, 1993), p. 83.

2 <www.christiancourier.com/articles/282-jesus-and-the-samaritan-woman>

3 <www.theatlantic.com/technology/archive/2020/01/tweeting-talmud/604366/>

4 <www.huffpost.com/entry/should-i-thank-god-for-not-making-me-a-woman_b_3197422>

5 R. Gamble, *Jesus the Evangelist* (David C. Cook, Eastbourne, 2009), p. 229.

6 M. Gladwell, *Talking to Strangers* (Little, Brown, New York, 2019), p. i.

9 × (multiply) – Moses had a mentor . . . and an apprentice

1 <www.theguardian.com/commentisfree/2018/oct/19/ageism-greedy-oldies-brexit-young-people>

2 R. A. Kenny, *Age Proof* (Lagom, London, 2022), p. 28.

3 <www.ageuk.org.uk/globalassets/age-uk/documents/reports-and-publications/reports-and-briefings/health--wellbeing/rb_june15_lonelines_in_later_life_evidence_review.pdf>

4 J. Yates, *Fractured* (HarperNorth, Manchester, 2021), p. 20.

5 S. Biddulph, *Raising Boys* (HarperCollins, London, 1997), p. 37.

6 L. Sweet, *11* (David C. Cook, Colorado Springs CO, 2008), p. 64.

7 D. Kinnaman and M. Matlock, *Faith for Exiles* (Baker Books, Grand Rapids MI, 2019), p. 138.

8 Kinnaman and Matlock, *Faith for Exiles*, p. 139.

9 J. C. Pollock, *Hudson Taylor and Maria* (Hodder & Stoughton, London, 1962), p. 61.

10 Sweet, *11*, p. 84.

10 + (add) – Moses had a God

1 A. W. Tozer, *The Knowledge of the Holy* (General Press, New Delhi, 2019), p. 5.

2 D. Willard, *Renovation of the Heart* (NavPress, Colorado Springs CO, 2002), p. 176.

3 D. Male and P. Weston, *The Word's Out* (BRF, Abingdon, 2013), p. 109.

Conclusion

1 <www.today.com/news/one-man-s-forgiveness-after-tragedy-creates-profound-friendship-stranger-t144626>

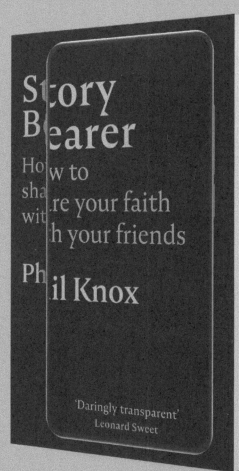

The Evangelical Alliance

The Evangelical Alliance is made up of hundreds of organizations, thousands of churches and tens of thousands of individuals, joined together for the sake of the gospel. Representing our members since 1846, the Evangelical Alliance is the oldest and largest evangelical unity movement in the UK.

United in mission and voice, we exist to serve and strengthen the work of the church in our communities and throughout society. Highlighting the significant opportunities and challenges facing the church today, we work together to resource Christians so that they are able to act upon their faith in Jesus, to speak up for the gospel, justice and freedom in their areas of influence.

Working across the UK, with offices in London, Cardiff, Glasgow and Belfast, our members come together from across denominations, locations, age groups and ethnicities, all sharing a passion to know Jesus and make him known.